Do The~~~~
You're Stupid?

100 Ways of Spotting Spin and Nonsense from the Media, Pundits and Politicians

Julian Baggini

GRANTA

Granta Publications, 12 Addison Avenue, London W11 4QR

First published in Great Britain as *The Duck that Won the Lottery:
And 99 Other Bad Arguments* by Granta Books, 2008
This paperback edition published by Granta Books, 2010

A CIP catalogue record for this book
is available from the British Library.

3 5 7 9 10 8 6 4 2

ISBN 978 1 84708 083 7

Printed and bound in Great Britain by
CPI Group (UK) Ltd, Croydon, CR0 4YY

Contents

Contents

Contents

Contents

Contents

Contents

Preface

Doing things right is simple: just eliminate all your mistakes and then you'll be perfect. This is as true for thinking and arguing well as it is in any other skill. The main priority for someone who aspires to think clearly is to cut out all the fallacies and confusions that infect reasoning. The problem is that there are so many of them, and for better or worse, human beings are not Spock-like logicians.

This book sets out to highlight 100 common ways in which people argue badly. Most take their cue from examples of fallacious reasoning, but others focus on habits, styles and biases of thought. Others start from perfectly good arguments which are nonetheless used in unreasonable ways. It is not a textbook, and my list contains overlaps and variants of what logicians would identify as the same species of poor reasoning. I have chosen bad argumentative moves that are actually used in the real world, and have catalogued them accordingly, not necessarily in the same way as professors of philosophy and critical thinking. The cross-referencing is an invitation to explore the similarities and differences between the manoeuvres I describe.

Because the examples are drawn from real life, they reflect the issues that have, in recent years, provided the soil in which the weeds of unreason have grown most abundantly. Politics features prominently, in particular the response to terrorism and the war in Iraq. There are also multiple examples drawn from debates about environmentalism, alternative medicine, religion, abortion, euthanasia and poverty. And there are less serious examples, such as quantum sheep poets, lucky ducks and gods from outer space.

When I first had the idea for this book, I conceived it as a kind of offensive weapon in the war against nonsense. The reader could arm herself with it, then seek and destroy illogicality wherever it could be found. However, seeing other people engaged in such evangelical missions has made me think again. Good thinking is, I believe, less a matter of getting 'tooled up' and more a question of adopting an enquiring, sceptical – but not cynical – attitude. Over-confidence is one of reason's biggest enemies, all the more dangerous because it can emerge in its midst.

I have therefore tried to highlight some of the difficulties of applying even the clearest of critical thinking principles. At the end of each entry is a set of questions, a matter arising or a task that aims to give the reader something to chew over mentally after the book has been put down.

A book like this can easily give the impression that the line between the rational and the irrational is clear-cut, when, of course, it rarely is. Like its predecessor, *The Pig that Wants to Be Eaten*, this is intended as a starting point for better reasoning, not the last word on it.

A note (and apology) on examples used

Few would like to have their words used to illustrate bad arguments. However, I wanted to use real-life examples, so I fear I may have made 100 or so new enemies with this book.

Please, however, bear a few things in mind. First, on several occasions, the quote I start with is not itself an example of sloppy thinking, but is commonly used as the basis of some poor reasoning. Second, in some cases I make it very clear that, although their precise words are clear examples of what generally are bad arguments, in context there may be good reasons why they were nonetheless used. Third, I have not chosen people according to whether I generally agree or disagree with them. Part of my purpose is to show that bad arguments are made by our friends as well as our foes, in support of things we agree with as well as those we disagree with. Fourth, I am sure that if someone else had written this book, they could have picked on something I have said. I call 'foul' knowing that when I'm playing instead of refereeing, I too am guilty of infringements.

Having said that, some people deserve all the criticism they get.

All the primary sources are listed at the back of the book. In the main text, when I have given the position of the person I am quoting it is generally that which they held at the time they made their comment.

Acknowledgements

This book grew out of a series called *Bad Moves* which I wrote for *ButterfliesandWheels.com*. I am indebted to Jeremy Stangroom and Ophelia Benson for giving me this opportunity and for providing critical editorial comment on the columns. This book is now several steps removed from that series and any errors or infelicities are entirely my responsibility.

At Granta, I'd like to thank George Miller for commissioning the book before he moved on to pastures new, and Sara Holloway for taking it on. Thanks also to Bela Cunha, Julio Ferrandis, Brigid Macleod, Lindsay Paterson, Angela Rose, Pru Rowlandson, Christine Lo and Sarah Wasley.

Finally, thanks to Antonia for all the support in the months when finishing this book could have got in the way of everything but, thanks to her, didn't.

1. I just don't believe it!

Arguments from incredulity

> No one in their right mind can look in the stars and the eternal blackness everywhere and deny the spirituality of the experience, nor the existence of a Supreme Being.
>
> Eugene Cernan, last man on the moon[1]

No one in their right mind could read Cernan's testimony and deny that NASA must be giving its astronauts training in advanced rhetoric. In just one sentence, Cernan manages to pack three dubious, but persuasive, punches. There's the personal, *ad hominem* abuse – people who disagree are just not in 'their right mind'. There's also a whiff of the argument from authority, an 'I've been into space, buddy, and you haven't, so you'd better believe I know what I'm talking about' attitude. And at the core, what can be called the argument from incredulity.

An argument from incredulity essentially works by taking the fact that one can't believe or imagine that something is true (or false) to be a good reason for thinking it isn't true (or false).

In this case, when he looks into space, Cernan simply can't believe that there isn't some kind of spiritual dimension or supreme being behind it all. The implicit argument buried beneath this assertion is that because he cannot look out into space and deny the existence of a supreme being, and no other sane person could either, therefore, it follows the supreme being is real.

And that really is the sum total of his case. He makes it sound as though you too should be equally unable to deny the deity by claiming you're not in your right mind if you do deny it. But that's just an assertion mixed up with some abuse. It doesn't advance the argument any further.

As is often the case with a bad argument, once its structure is made explicit, its weaknesses become obvious. Our own inability to imagine that something is or is not the case is not in itself a reason to think it is or is not the case. Some true things just are unimaginable. And the fact that we have strong convictions when confronted by certain experiences does not mean that those convictions are reliable bases for true belief.

Even if Cernan is right about what it is possible to deny, all that would show is something about the limits of human credulity, not the existence or otherwise of things certain experiences compel us to believe.

There are plenty of examples of cases where we would be rash to make too much of our own imaginative limits. I can't really imagine the evolution of life from single cells to human beings, but I should not think my inability to imagine this provides some kind of reason for thinking evolution is not how humans came to be. More obviously, when I see a magician chop a person in two, I can't see how the trick works, but I would be foolish to think that the person had in fact been sawn in half.

However, even though an argument from incredulity looks like an open and shut case of sloppy thinking, at its core is an uncomfortable truth about the fundamental limits of human reason. There always comes a point in a rational argument where you just have to *see* that something is the case. If I've explained to you what numbers are, and how addition works, you just see that $1 + 1 = 2$. I can explain things again if you haven't got it, but at some point the truth of the sum will strike you as obvious and undeniable. Similarly, if I show you experiments that prove, say, the law of gravity, at some stage you just have to 'get it'.

What's the difference between someone in their right mind looking into the cosmos and denying the existence of a supreme being, and someone in their right mind looking at 1+1 and denying it makes 2? Aren't some perceptions of the divine so real to some people that they can no more disavow them than they can the existence of their own minds? If we accept that 'we can't deny it' never justifies the further claim 'it is true', aren't we condemned to universal scepticism?

See also

2. Quantum leaping sheep

Spurious science

I decided to explore randomness and some of the principles of quantum mechanics, through poetry, using the medium of sheep.

Valerie Laws, text artist and poet [2]

It's all too easy to mock contemporary art, especially when ruminating mammals are involved. Valerie Laws sprayed one word on the back of each member of a flock of sheep, using a total of seventeen syllables, the same number as in a traditional Japanese haiku. The idea was that the sheep would constantly rearrange themselves, each time creating a new poem, which would exist for just as long as the sheep remained still.

I am sure there are many who share her delight in lambic pentameter, but what has this got to do with quantum mechanics? Quantum theory explains the workings of only the very smallest parts of the universe, at the sub-atomic level. The idea that sheep can 'utilize' quantum principles while meandering around a field is about as muddle-headed as you can get.

'Quantum mechanics is a branch of physics which a lot of people find hard to understand, as it seems to go against common sense,' said Laws, before going on to prove her point by example. 'Randomness and uncertainty is at the centre of how the universe is put together, and is quite difficult for us as humans who rely on order.'

Laws seemed to have latched on to a few buzz-words associated with quantum theory – randomness and uncertainty – as though they captured what is particular about it. But the uncertainty of quantum mechanics concerns the speed and position of electrons and the impossibility of measuring both simultaneously. There is, however, no problem in ascertaining the speed and position of the sheep. The poems they form may be random, but randomness has no particular connection with the principles of quantum mechanics. Randomness, at least at some level of description, is a phenomenon that appears in other areas of the physical sciences.

All kinds of science can be misused in similar ways, but it is the spurious adoption of quantum theory to make something sound more impressive which has reached epidemic proportions. There is, for instance, a lot of talk about 'quantum consciousness': explaining consciousness by the use of quantum theory. There is some serious research here and Roger Penrose, for example, has argued that he believes the solution to the problem of consciousness will come from quantum theory. But the vast majority of the 'literature' on this is just a combination of speculation and dubious analogy. So, for example, Danah Zohar in *The Quantum Self*, speculates that the quantum wave/particle duality corresponds to the duality between the physical and the mental. The reasoning seems to be that particles are a bit concrete and so like the physical, and waves are more fluffy and thus more like the mental. This analogy added to a liberal dose of speculation leads to her explaining consciousness as the fusing of the two in quantum states of the brain, even though almost all physicists think that the kind of quantum state Zohar thinks explains consciousness – the Bose-Einstein condensate – could not exist in something as warm and wet as the brain.[3]

Quantum mechanics is difficult and hard to understand, so people seem to think that anything else difficult and hard to understand should somehow be seen as a quantum phenomenon. But this adds up to no explanation at all. As the psychologist Susan Blackmore said in a report on a conference at which these theories were offered as explanations for consciousness, '. . . they didn't explain it. They quantummed it.'[4]

The spurious use of quantum theory is an example of another bad argumentative move: substituting one mystery for another, as though that were an explanation. I wonder, however, if some very popular ideas also fall under this description. For instance, is the mystery of Creation explained by positing a mysterious God, beyond our comprehension, as the first cause? As well as the misuse of science to explain things, isn't there a misuse of religion to explain what science cannot?

See also

3. Cheese-eating surrender monkeys

Selective quotation

My position is that, regardless of the circumstances, France will vote 'no'.

Jacques Chirac, president of France[5]

When Groundskeeper Willie in *The Simpsons* called the French 'cheese-eating surrender monkeys', it was surely a send-up rather than a celebration of the then mood of francophobia. But the phrase was happily adopted by many Americans and Britons who were unimpressed by the French stance on Saddam Hussein.

It wasn't just the matter of their opposing the war on Iraq – many countries did that – it was the manner in which they appeared to do so. What more than anything enabled critical commentators to paint the French as unreasonable in their opposition was President Chirac's declaration in a television interview that 'regardless of the circumstances', France would exercise its veto and vote against any 'second' UN resolution on Iraq. (In fact, Downing Street lists ten previous resolutions on Iraq, including 1441, which it claims Iraq had not fully complied with.) The remark caused outrage in Britain and America – evidence, it was said, that France had closed its ears to reason and argument. Downing Street called it 'poisonous' and Jack Straw, the foreign secretary, said it had made war more likely.

Chirac, however, was the victim of selective quotation. What he actually said, in full, was: 'My position is that, regardless of the circumstances, France will vote "no" because she considers this evening that there are no grounds for waging war in order to achieve the goal we have set ourselves, i.e. to disarm Iraq.'

The crucial words here are 'this evening'. Even more importantly, the discussion prior to these comments had clearly been about how France would vote that evening (if there had been a vote), in a number of different hypothetical circumstances, such as there being or not being a majority of nine on the Security Council for a new resolution. So 'regardless of the circumstances' clearly meant regardless of how other members of the Council voted, and 'this evening' indicated that the stance being taken was not one that would never be changed.

Indeed, Chirac explicitly did not rule out the eventual use of force. 'France isn't a pacifist country,' he said, and it 'doesn't refuse war on principle. France considers that war is the final stage of a process.'

However, by selectively quoting Chirac – pulling out a short phrase and not even a whole sentence – he could be portrayed as an implacable opponent of the use of force under all conceivable circumstances. In other words, a cheese-eating surrender monkey.

This crime is not to be confused with the inevitable and harmless practice of quoting only short extracts or phrases. In this sense, anything other than a full reprint of the original speech or work is selective quotation, and every entry in this book begins with a selective quotation. The phrase 'selective quotation' implies a distortion, so when a selection does not misrepresent the speaker, it should not be so named.

There are some areas where the issue of whether something has been done violence by selective quotation is hotly disputed. Many who follow the Bible or the Qu'ran, for example, claim that certain passages seem morally objectionable only because they are quoted out of context. Others counter that they say exactly what they appear to say.

So what are we to make of this passage from the Qu'ran, which relates to witnessing of contracts with debtors: 'And call in to witness two witnesses, men; or if the two be not men, then one man and two women, such witnesses as you approve of, that if one of the two women errs the other will remind her; and let the witnesses not refuse, whenever they are summoned' (Sura 2:282). And is there any ambiguity in the words of Jesus in Matthew: 'Do not suppose that I have come to bring peace to the earth. I did not come to bring peace, but a sword. For I have come to turn a man against his father, a daughter against her mother, a daughter-in-law against her mother-in-law – a man's enemies will be the members of his own household' (10:34-26). Are these selective quotations or merely revealing ones?

See also

4. Que será, será

'If I don't, somebody else will'

> If we want to stop the defence industry operating in this country, we can do so. The result incidentally would be that someone else supplies the arms that we supply.
>
> Tony Blair[6]

How many times have we heard people justifying ethically dubious actions using this kind of argumentative move? The logic is clear enough: my action has a consequence which you find objectionable. But if I don't undertake that action, someone else will, and so that consequence will still come about. So there's no point in criticizing me for doing it, because that won't prevent the consequence you object to from coming to pass.

Consequentialist moral theories agree that an action is wrong if it has bad consequences and right if it has good ones. But that doesn't mean an action becomes right just because someone else will do it anyway.

If this mistake is clear enough, why then does the argument have a curious appeal? One reason is plain wishful thinking combined with self-interest. We most often use or hear this kind of argument when someone has something to lose by not doing the dubious action, or something to gain by doing it. Therefore pure self-interest can make us cling to any justification that seems to make our action justifiable.

A second explanation is more charitable to those who invoke such arguments. It is natural and probably right to think that the morality of actions is in some way tied to how they contribute or do not contribute to making the world a better place. So in some sense the question, 'Will the world be any better if I do or do not do this?' is a perfectly good one to ask. But in answering it we need to think not only about the net result of our actions when combined with those of others, but also about our contribution to that result. It may well be that the world will not be any better if I refrain from doing something bad. But if it is I who does that bad thing rather than someone else, then I am the one who is responsible for what happens. I am not less responsible because someone else would have done it. The fact is that I *did* do it and so must carry the blame.

This is in fact how we usually judge people morally. For instance, imagine a group of your friends plot to kill someone and they cannot be dissuaded. Does that mean that if you then volunteered to be the assassin, you would be blameless, because someone was going to pull the trigger anyway? The idea is surely absurd.

When it comes to arms dealing, the fact that if Britain doesn't do it other countries will is not a sufficient justification. What we need to know is whether the arms dealing is morally justifiable in itself. Like magicians' tricks, the argument fools us into looking away from where the real sleight of hand is taking place.

The plea is occasionally at least worth taking seriously, particularly when refusing to do wrong has repercussions for the refusenik. In countless repressive regimes people have been tortured, raped and even exterminated in death camps. For any given individual involved in those atrocities, it is almost always the case that if they hadn't done it, someone else would have. But that does not make their actions permissible. We may feel some sympathy for people who were forced to choose between undertaking horrible acts and being punished or even killed themselves, but these are factors which mitigate our judgement of the wrongdoer; they do not render the wrongdoing right.

Is it ever a good defence to argue that it is better that you do something wrong than someone else do it, with even graver consequences? What, for example, if the choice is between supplying pure heroin legally or leaving it to criminals who care less about contamination? Isn't there at least something in the plea that if I don't do it, someone else will, with even worse consequences?

See also

5. Speak for yourself

The existentialist fallacy

> By killing herself, she was saying that life as a disabled person is not worth living.
>
> Gillian Gerhardi, disabled mother of two[7]

In January 2006, Dr Anne Turner travelled to the Swiss Dignitas clinic to end her own life. The 66-year-old had the degenerative brain disease progressive supranuclear palsy (PSP). She slurred her speech badly, had trouble swallowing, could no longer take a bath unaided and had difficulty feeding her cats. Both her husband and her brother had died from similar conditions and Dr Turner did not want to suffer the same fate.

Opponents of euthanasia seemed to be particularly disturbed by Dr Turner's case because she had relatively few symptoms and still had years to live. The Bishop of Oxford, the Right Reverend Richard Harries, said we should never help someone to end their life, and if someone decided that's what they wanted, 'I would want to try to convince them that even if they got into a state where they were very dependent and felt very helpless and useless, their life was still precious.'[8] What he didn't say, but implied, was that if he failed to convince them, he would not want them to carry out their wishes anyway.

Euthanasia is a very difficult moral issue, and an even greater legal one. Even if you think that one has the moral right to end one's own life (as I do), the consequences of legislation have to be thought through very carefully. One serious worry is that by making it easier for people to end their own lives, those whose illnesses make them depend on others may increasingly feel that they are placing an unfair burden on people, and may choose to die, even though it is not what they really want.

A related issue is how euthanasia, coupled with the abortion of foetuses showing signs of disability, might strengthen the view that the life of a disabled person is not worth living. This could have real consequences for the disabled, who have fought hard to make society see that they can lead happy, worthwhile lives.

Against this background, I would not like to be too harsh on Gillian Gerhardi. Her reaction to Dr Turner's suicide is hardly likely to be positive. Dr Turner 'wasn't anywhere near as bad as I am', she said. But I'm afraid Gerhardi was wrong when she went on to say, 'Yes, her brain disorder meant she was going to deteriorate, but by killing herself, she was saying that life as a disabled person is not worth living.' Not at all. Turner had merely decided that she did not judge her own life worth living, not that others in similar circumstances might decide otherwise.

Yet Gerhardi's logic seems compelling to many. Why is that? There are several possibilities. One is that people assume that there have to be objective, factual answers to questions about the sanctity of life. A certain type of life must either be worth living or not. If that assumption were right, then it would be true that anyone deciding their life was not worth living would indeed be saying the same of all similar kinds of life. But this is not the only way to see the issue at all. The alternative is to say that the value of life is at least in part subjective, and that we are free ourselves to determine whether, in our own cases, life is worth living or not. Someone who makes a decision on this assumption is not guilty of saying that what is true for them is true for others.

I've called this the existentialist fallacy because it echoes something Sartre once said: 'When I choose for myself I choose for all mankind.'[9] Taken literally, that might seem to back up Gerhardi. But I think that what he really meant was that when I choose for myself, I *legitimate* that choice for all mankind. In other words, Dr Turner's decision implied that she thought others were *entitled* to do the same, not that they *must* do so. Confuse these two, and you commit the fallacy.

Identifying the logical error in this example still leaves a huge moral question unsolved: is the value of life something that we can decide for ourselves, or is it actually an objective matter? This is the deeper problem that many religious people have with euthanasia. It is not just what we choose to do, it is that we dare to decide what is of ultimate value. Are they right, or do we have to make our own minds up about these big issues, whether we believe God has the final answers or not?

See also

6. The amazing psychic poet

Confirmation bias

> [Jonathan Cainer] met a psychic poet called Charles John Quatro, who told him he would some day write an astrology column read by millions.
>
> David Smith, *Observer*[10]

And would you believe it, many years later, Jonathan Cainer does write an astrology column read by millions! Incidentally, Cainer's predictions grace the pages of 'a newspaper dedicated to the subtle propagation of bigotry'. That description of the *Daily Mail* is by, ahem, Jonathan Cainer, when working for a more left-wing paper.

Are you impressed by the uncanny accuracy of Quatro's prediction? Let me make my own predictions: if you already believe in astrology, your answer will be 'yes'. If you don't, your answer will be 'no'. If you're agnostic, you will probably find it somewhat impressive.

Was I right? Probably, though not because I possess any psychic powers. Rather, I am simply aware of an effect psychologists call 'confirmation bias'. This concerns how we filter out the mass of evidence for or against various theories and hypotheses, and consider evidence that supports what we already believe to be stronger or more significant than that which undermines it. Indeed, we may go so far as to pay little or no attention at all to contrary evidence and focus our attention almost exclusively on that which bolsters our prior convictions.

This helps explain why so many people are impressed by the claims of psychics and astrologers. If we are inclined to believe in the supernatural, then it is easy to focus on those examples where predictions come true, or where psychics make accurate statements about the past or present. These 'confirm' our beliefs that they really do have access to a source of knowledge beyond the physical world, or at least the world as science understands it.

If we do not believe in the supernatural, however, we will focus on the countless times when predictions are wrong or when psychics make mistakes. Reading the article about Jonathan Cainer, for example – setting aside doubts about the truth of the story – we will think that this one accurate prediction doesn't count for much, for the psychic probably also said many other things that were not true.

It should be clear, therefore, that people on both sides of the debate can fall victim to confirmation bias. However, it should also be clear that, in this case, confirmation bias works more to the benefit of believers than sceptics. This is because if we try to take a genuinely balanced look at the evidence, we will find that for every apparent instance of a true prediction by an astrologer there are many other false ones. What is more, many predictions are so vague that it is always possible to say that they came true in some sense. Confirmation bias is thus more likely to lead the believer into error because the balance of evidence does stack up against the truth of astrology. It is only by selecting the evidence to fit their beliefs that they could possibly come to the conclusion that astrology works.

Confirmation bias infects political discourse too. It is almost certainly the case that, once they were persuaded that Iraq had WMD, Blair and Bush placed more weight on evidence that supported their position than that which challenged it. They may have tried to keep open minds, but, once you have committed yourself to what you see as the truth, it becomes very hard to assess all the evidence impartially.

On the other side, those who are persuaded that Bush and Blair were driven by purely selfish motives are much more impressed by evidence that supports this view than that which suggests that they might have been sincere, even if mistaken. The genuinely open question of whether they lied or were mistaken about WMD becomes an open and shut case in the face of 'clear' evidence that they lied, while any counter-evidence is dismissed.

Confirmation bias is a real impediment to good thinking but, unlike some errors in reasoning, it is very hard to root out. Where are you most prone to it? Are you more receptive to the claims made for organic food than those against, or the other way around? Are you on the lookout for evidence that we are or are not destroying the planet? Do you spot the signs that your child is especially talented more than you do those which suggest he or she is quite average?

See also

7. Because I say so

Truth by stipulation

'We are concerned that the Government may have drawn back from a whole-hearted commitment to meeting the 2010–11 target. A failure to meet that target would represent a conscious decision to leave hundreds of thousands of children in poverty for longer than is necessary or desirable.'

House of Commons Treasury Select Committee[11]

The British government has set ambitious targets to halve child poverty by 2010 and abolish it altogether by 2020. Since it made that pledge, 600,000 children have been taken out of poverty. But in 2005–6 there was a serious setback and the number actually rose by 200,000. Taking housing costs into account, the Joseph Rowntree Foundation calculated that in 2005 one in three children still lived below the poverty line.[12]

But what exactly does 'child poverty' mean? Officially, it is defined as children living in a household on less than 60 per cent of median income. I'm sure it's true that at the moment children living in such conditions are genuinely deprived, and that society should do what it can to improve their lot. The problem I have is that, with the way poverty is defined, we could well end up in a few decades' time with 'poor children' eating well, in comfortable houses, with iPods, mobile phones and satellite televisions. Just as long as their household income was the right fraction of the average, we would have to say they were poor.

Even more absurd is the fact that the best way to reduce child poverty on this measure would be to reduce average incomes while maintaining those of the poorest in society. It is even logically possible that everyone in society could become worse off in absolute terms, but as long as the standard of living of the poorest declined the least, fewer of them would be officially poor. Paradoxically, more poverty would mean less 'poverty'.

This kind of nonsense often occurs when we stop using language in its natural, organic way and simply stipulate with great rigidity how certain terms should be used. It is inevitable that it happens, especially with governments, because they need to define strictly the terms they use in order to provide consistent measures. But it can have bizarre consequences. For instance, the MacPherson Report, the result of an inquiry set up after the murder of black teenager Stephen Lawrence, decided that a racial incident should be defined as 'any incident which is perceived to be racist by the victim or by any other person'. That means that if you hit me and I perceive that to be racially motivated, then the incident becomes a racial one, even if race had nothing to do with it.

We can stipulate whatever we want: if we're interested in truth we need to know whether that stipulation is a fair one. Official definitions, however, fix 'the truth' regardless of the reality.

The way in which the definition of poverty has been stipulated means that, realistically speaking, we will never abolish it. Recent UNICEF figures on child poverty (in this case defined as households with less than 50 per cent of median national income) showed that even Sweden, which is among the top twenty richest countries in the world while at the same time being the third most equal, has some child poverty – 2.6 per cent, the lowest figure in the world.[13] It will always be true by stipulation that some children are poor, even if they have everything they need to enjoy healthy, long and fulfilled lives.

There is an argument that inequality will always matter, no matter how rich we all become. That may be right, but it does not follow that it will always be accurate to say that having less than 60 per cent of median income makes you poor.

Many striking claims are made which are based on dubious definitions. It is therefore important that whether it is true people fall into these categories or not does not just depend on how we choose to stipulate their meaning. For example, can the EU's current stipulation of what makes food 'fresh' make any sense when it applies to meat which can be months old? More seriously, according to the UNHCR's definition of a refugee, many women who flee their countries because of repeated rape are not refugees because rape is not political persecution. Is that right? The definition of 'homeless' is also contested. Many people think it applies only to people who sleep rough, but those in temporary accommodation are also usually counted. So what should count as genuinely being homeless?

See also

8. Don't misunderestimate me

Lack of charity

> Reports that say that something hasn't happened are always interesting to me, because as we know, there are known knowns; there are things we know we know. We also know there are known unknowns; that is to say we know there are some things we do not know. But there are also unknown unknowns — the ones we don't know we don't know.

Donald Rumsfeld, US Defense Secretary[14]

The verbal virtuosity of Donald Rumsfeld is legendary. 'We do know of certain knowledge that he [Osama Bin Laden] is either in Afghanistan, or in some other country, or dead.' Genius. 'I believe what I said yesterday. I don't know what I said, but I know what I think, and, well, I assume it's what I said.' Reassuring. 'I also know that stating what might be preferable is simply stating what might be preferable.' Revelatory.

The combination of his oral awkwardness and neo-con politics made Rumsfeld fair game during his stint as US Defense Secretary. In most circles, there was only one way of talking about him: negatively.

Rumsfeld-bashing reached its zenith in the UK when the Plain English Campaign awarded him the 'Foot in Mouth' award for the most baffling comment by a public figure. It was, of course, for his notorious 'known unknowns' remark. However, there is one problem: his remarks made perfect sense. His distinction between known knowns, known unknowns and unknown unknowns is entirely logical and worthy of a philosophy major.

Known knowns include the distance from the earth to the moon, the chemical structure of water and the capital of Belgium. Known unknowns include how brains give rise to consciousness, the composition of dark matter and the whereabouts of Lord Lucan. Unknown unknowns are all the other things that are the case but we do not yet, or never will, know about. Before 1930, for example, Pluto was an unknown unknown.

If it was so coherent, why did Rumsfeld's remark get so widely mocked? One reason is because we did not extend the principle of charity to him, as we do to people we have sympathy for. The principle of charity has nothing to do with donating money. Rather, it is the methodological principle that determines that, when trying to make sense of what someone else is saying, we give it the most favourable interpretation possible. Put another way, it is trying to give people the benefit of the doubt with regard to the coherence of their utterances. Even if you think that Rumsfeld lost the right to be given the benefit of the doubt years ago, there are reasons for generally extending this courtesy even to those we strongly disagree with.

One is that we know people sometimes choose the wrong words but it's usually not hard to know what they mean. If a barman is asked for a 'peanut colada' for example, it would be very cruel of him to prepare a nut-based cocktail. At the very least, he should check if peanuts are really what the customer is after.

Perhaps the most important reason for being charitable is that the best you can do with an uncharitable interpretation is dismiss someone's comments. But if you take the best interpretation possible, you might just get hold of something worth discussing. This is true even if, in fact, the person's thoughts were nonsense after all. The principle does not say that people always mean what the most coherent interpretation of what they say is, only that it is better, in general, to assume they do, unless proven otherwise.

You can, of course, give someone too much benefit of the doubt. So how much is the right amount to give? Consider Tony Blair's comments about his decision to go to war: 'I think if you have faith about these things, then you realize that that judgement is made by other people, and if you believe in God, it's made by God as well.' Blair was widely pilloried for bringing God into the debate, but wasn't he just being honest about what any Christian would believe? And are these comments by the singer Morrissey straight observations or the words of a racist: 'Travel to England and you have no idea where you are . . . If you walk through Knightsbridge you'll hear every accent apart from an English accent.' Does either man deserve the benefit of the doubt?

See also

9. Tap water is for plants

Getting it out of proportion

Drinking around three litres of pure still filtered water a day makes a vital contribution to health.

Emma Mitchell, *Guardian*[15]

For several years, 'natural health therapist' Emma Mitchell gave advice on how to live a healthier life in a weekly column for the *Guardian*. Mitchell was usually pretty sensible, and her advice to drink more water is in line with recommendations from most health experts. However, no mention of H_2O was complete for Mitchell without the qualifying word 'filtered' attached. Filtering, she said, 'helps eliminate toxins'.

She's probably right, but I suspect that filtering water provides such an insignificant benefit that to think one ought to do it for the sake of one's own health is akin to thinking one can increase one's life expectancy by exercising for ninety-one minutes per week rather than ninety.

Certainly the British Drinking Water Inspectorate thinks so. They insist that 'All public water supplies in England and Wales are safe to drink and there is no need to install additional treatment within the home as a health protection measure.' And they claim that strict controls on levels of pesticides mean 'additional filtration is not required'. A recent report found that 99.96 per cent of water samples met legal standards and none of those that failed posed a health risk.

The Consumers Association also concluded in a report that tap water, filtered or unfiltered, often tasted better than bottled water, and that no water source contained unsafe levels of bacteria.

In the US, it seems that tap water quality is more variable. But even the Natural Resources Defense Council, which campaigns for better quality tap water, thinks that it is usually unnecessary to filter water.

Such is the insignificance of the health benefits of filtered water that not even its manufacturers make strong claims for it. The UK market leader Brita, for example, focuses its marketing on the general benefits of drinking water and only on the taste improvements it claims its filters provide. It also openly acknowledges that its cartridges cannot remove nitrates, reassuring us that 'Water companies have to comply with the standards set down in the EC water quality regulations.' But if these standards are good enough for what the filters can't remove, then surely they are good enough for what they can.

To think, therefore, that one really owes it to one's heath to bother to filter tap water when the tapped supply is perfectly decent is to get things out of proportion. Unfortunately, such losses of proportion are all too common, as we are generally very bad at assessing risks and tend to worry far too much about things that are of little importance or over which we have no control, and ignore the basics of diet and exercise that really can affect both life expectancy and quality of life. Ironically, paranoia about issues such as drinking-water may fuel the kind of stress which might finish you off prematurely.

Arguably, this isn't just an intellectual and prudential mistake but a moral one. To worry about the infinitesimally small increase in risk to one's health from drinking unfiltered water or eating fruit with minuscule pesticide traces when one billion people do not have access to safe water and when a child dies every fifteen seconds from water–related diseases looks like moral myopia at its most narcissistic. That is why when I returned from a trip to East Africa, where young children were frequently seen carrying jerry cans for miles, I threw my water filter out in disgust. (However, I soon replaced it when I discovered that my unfiltered water just didn't taste nice. Which goes to show how even though one reason for doing something might be bad, there might be another good reason for doing exactly the same thing anyway.)

It's not always easy to spot which side of a debate is most guilty of getting things out of proportion. Who is more guilty of lack of perspective: those who turn against all things green because they get so fed up with the excessive righteousness of environmentalists, or sanctimonious eco-warriors themselves? Is pseudo-science more of a problem than excessive reliance on science, or vice versa?

See also

10. Sexy like me

Automorphism

> The forests of the world hum up the erotic . . . nature swells with sex.
>
> Jay Griffiths, *Wild*[16]

Anthropomorphism is everywhere. When human beings invent gods, they are almost always gendered hominoids like us, only bigger, more powerful and harder to get hold of on the phone. Even gods with animal forms have plenty of human characteristics. We also give names to animals themselves, and some even receive presents at Christmas. We can't help but see dolphins as smiling and Bernese mountain dogs as having doleful eyes.

Most of the time this is all quite harmless. But Disneyesque anthropomorphism is just a subset of a wider, more insidious bias we have towards automorphism: seeing other things in our own image. If this were as easy to spot as the artifice of Mickey Mouse, we'd have no problem, but it tends to creep up on us much less noticeably.

In her award-winning book *Wild*, Jay Griffiths seems to make this mistake when she views nature as being inherently, uncontrollably sexual, using phrases like 'nature swells with sex' and 'wilderness and wild nature are sexual'. Her prose is breathless, passionate, but – though I feel like a killjoy pointing this out – highly misleading.

First of all, much of nature just isn't sexual – it's positively asexual. Griffiths herself provides an example when she illustrates the supposed eroticism of the forest by describing 'moss, damp and steaming'. But moss reproduces asexually, as do non-flowering plants and single-cell organisms.

Most of the rest is neither sexual nor asexual but inert. More than two-thirds of the planet is covered by sea which contains lots of life but is itself just a chemical compound. Add to that rocks, soil, sand and air and you have a lot of stuff which is biologically dead.

Second, even animals that reproduce sexually are generally not in heat most of the time. Griffiths recalls how with the help of a shaman and ayahuasca, a psychoactive drug, she shape-shifted into a jaguar. 'Sexual desire was streaming through me,' she wrote of the effects of the N-dimethyltryptamine, and 'Sex glistened me, every cell of me.' She must have caught the feline on an unusually horny day: jaguars have a thirty-seven-day reproductive cycle and are in heat for only half that time. Dogs mate during only two periods of the year. Bears, foxes and wolves are at it only in the spring.

Third, and most importantly, animal sex usually has little in common with human eroticism. Most animal intercourse lasts for seconds and is not preceded by any foreplay. It is true that some species show signs of sexual play, but this is the exception not the rule. Even when nature is sexual, it is usually not at all erotic.

I suspect that Griffiths's description of nature is more than just anthropomorphic, it is automorphic. In the book it becomes very evident that she is a deeply sensuous person. She then seems to project this on to the world: because nature evokes a strong sensuous response in her, she thinks that it must be sensuous too.

That said, the flipside of automorphism is hardly less dangerous. The failure to see common characteristics between us and others is not just a logical mistake, it can lead to moral horrors. Throughout human history, people have refused to accept that those of different ethnic origin, or even gender, were really like themselves. The result turns people into things and that can lead to the most appalling abuse. Automorphism should therefore be seen not as the polar opposite of the right way of seeing things but as one of two extremes. We should strive to strike a balance between seeing too much of ourselves in others and not seeing enough.

Thinking straight about how like us others are is particularly important when it comes to assessing how continuous we are with other animals. Most people now accept that there is no absolute human/animal divide, but disagree as to the extent of the overlap. Many animals communicate, but is it anthropomorphic to say that they use language? Do we kid ourselves if we say that the sensations animals feel are not sufficiently like human pain for us to take them into account? Which is the greater error: seeing too much of the human in animals, or too little of the animal in ourselves?

See also

11. Eat up your GMs

Non sequiturs

As yet another (British) panel concluded this week, there is no evidence that GM crops now in commercial cultivation are more dangerous to human health than conventional foods. So there is no reason why Europeans should not eat the GM food that Americans already consume by the siloful.

Economist[17]

In the broad sense, most bad arguments are varieties of *non sequiturs*: conclusions that are drawn but which do not follow. Saddam Hussein showed himself to be a brilliant exponent of the *non sequitur* in his surreal interview with British parliamentarian Tony Benn. In this short exchange he used the word 'therefore' six times, in every case either introducing a *non sequitur* or drawing a banal, self-evident conclusion ('Therefore we are facing a critical situation'). Here's the best example:

Those people and others have been telling the various US administrations, especially the current one, that if you want to control the world you need to control the oil. Therefore the destruction of Iraq is a pre-requisite to controlling oil.

The important thing about *non sequiturs* is that what is at issue is not necessarily the truth of the main claims being made, but the inferential connection between them. For example, if I say, 'I like cheese, therefore it's Tuesday,' I have uttered a *non sequitur*, since the fact that it is Tuesday doesn't follow from the fact that I like cheese. But it may nevertheless be true both that it is Tuesday and I do like cheese. Similarly, the fact that Saddam uttered a *non sequitur* does not in itself prove that the US did not want to control the world's oil, nor that they didn't see the destruction of Iraq as a means of achieving their goal; it is simply that the latter doesn't follow from the former. But people do seem to like scattering their texts with 'therefore' and 'so' whether or not there is any logical connection between the claims these words link.

The *Economist's non sequitur* is that it does not follow from the fact that a British panel has concluded that GM foods are safe to eat that there is no reason not to eat them. Many people are opposed to GM foods for non-health reasons, such as their alleged threat to bio-diversity, the power they give agribusiness, or for fear that we just don't know what the long-term effects of wide-scale genetic manipulation of crops will be.

In defence of the *Economist*, newspaper articles are not formal arguments with clearly defined premises and conclusions. Most journalistic arguments are *enthymemes* – ones which rest on unstated, often assumed, premises.

It doesn't take too much digging to identify the enthymematic nature of the *Economist* leader. The first words – 'As yet another (British) panel concluded' – suggest that we should assume the premise that there has been plenty of research into the health risks of GM food, enough research to draw a conclusion from, and that all this research points the same way.

Similarly, the conclusion leaves a little out. We should take 'no reason why Europeans should not eat GM food' to mean no *health* reason, since those kinds of reasons are the only ones under consideration at this point.

Once we accept these implied facts, the *non sequitur* disappears. It does follow from the fact that lots of research – enough for us to trust the results – says that GM food is safe, that there is no good health reason not to eat it. Since the *Economist* prides itself on the clarity of its arguments, I don't feel any compunction in pulling it up on this rare lapse.

It is sometimes too easy to identify bad argumentative moves in writing which is not produced for a readership of pedantic logicians. Is this very book sometimes guilty of identifying *non sequiturs* simply by ignoring the premises and assumptions which are obviously implied if only one cares to look? How many of the so-called bad arguments I describe could be saved if only their enthymematic nature were made plain? I'll let you be the judge of that.

See also

12. Feels mighty real

Percipi est esse

Muslims in Britain are suffering soaring levels of Islamophobia and discrimination based on their faith, rather than the colour of their skin, a report published today says. [. . .] Of British Muslims, 80 per cent said they had suffered Islamophobia.

Maxine Frith, *Independent*[18]

Percipi est esse is a (possibly ungrammatical) inversion of Bishop Berkeley's *esse est percipi*: to be is to be perceived. Whereas Berkeley's original was a metaphysical claim about the nature of reality, 'to be perceived is to be' neatly captures the everyday way in which people often slide from the fact that something is perceived to be the case to the greater claim that it actually is the case.

This happened in the *Independent*'s story about a report on the perception of Islamophobia among Muslims. It solely concerned whether Muslims felt as though they had been discriminated against on the basis of their religion, not whether they had been. However, the fact that there had been an increase in the number of Muslims who thought they had been so discriminated against was taken as demonstrating that actual Islamophobia had increased. That was one giant illogical leap.

You need only consider other examples where the same inference could be made to see the flaw. Ask white Britons on council house waiting lists whether they feel they have been discriminated against in favour of asylum seekers and ethnic minorities, and you'll find a sizeable proportion believe they have, even when the facts show this is demonstrably not the case. If a newspaper were to report that discrimination against white working-class people had increased solely on the basis of the perceptions of this group, most would see the error in the logic and object straight away.

Given that this distinction is so clear, why do people fail to maintain it? I would conjecture that there are two main reasons. One is that language misleads. To say 'I felt God's presence' logically implies that God was actually present, just as to say 'I saw the Eiffel Tower' implies that the monument you saw was the Eiffel Tower. But in both cases we are simplifying what a completely accurate, and hence more circumspect, report would say. A pedant would insist you say 'I felt as though God were present' or 'I saw what looked to me like the Eiffel Tower,' neither of which implies that what you thought you felt or saw was really there.

A second reason why we make this error is that often something's seeming to be there is a reliable indicator that it is actually there. For everyday purposes at least, if you think you saw the Eiffel Tower you probably did. But this is not true of other experiences. With God, since there is no reliable way to distinguish really feeling His presence from merely seeming to, we surely cannot say that the latter is a reliable indicator of the former, although many insist it is. And in the case of prejudice, even if it is true that on most occasions when people believe they are the victims of prejudice they really are, the evidence of perception is still not a reliable enough indicator that the prejudice is actually there.

Some important truths are so simple that rock songs can not only express them, but do so with greater clarity than more sophisticated prose. Radiohead's song 'There There', contains the line, 'Just 'cause you feel it, doesn't mean it's there.' Since I couldn't improve on this summary of the fallacy I want to describe, for my heading I fell back on an old trick: if you want to make your idea look cleverer than it is, use Latin. But, of course, just because if looks cleverer, it doesn't mean it is.

For some things in life, it is often thought that there is no distinction between appearance and reality. If you *feel* pain, for example, surely you *are* in pain. However, it is not so clear that our emotions are infallible in the same way. If you feel you are in love, does that mean you really are, or could you be merely infatuated? Is it possible to think we feel angry, when really we're jealous or resentful? How much can we trust our perceptions of our emotions?

See also

1.   Arguments from incredulity
32.   'It sends the wrong message'
55.   The no coincidence presumption
79.   It's terrible so it can't be true

13. Trial by wardrobe

Subtle undermining

> Ms. Clinton, dressed in a brown pantsuit and turquoise shirt and jewellery, walked into the room talking about 'areas of expertise,' to steelworkers.
>
> Jason Horowitz, *New York Observer*[19]

Forgive the pun, but clothes are not immaterial. William James went so far as to claim that 'In its widest possible sense . . . a man's self is the sum total of all that he can call his,' including 'his clothes'. What we wear can be significant.

Politicians understand the semiotics of clothing and often consider their wardrobe very carefully indeed. It's not therefore unreasonable for commentators to comment on their choices sometimes. When as experienced a politician as Hillary Clinton appeared before the Senate in July 2007 showing some cleavage, for example, she almost certainly did so for a reason, and the press duly speculated as to what that might be. Most concluded she was trying to foreground her femininity.

It would be harsh to deduce anything specifically about Jason Horowitz solely on the basis of his mention of Clinton's attire when she met steelworkers. Perhaps he was simply drawing out the contrast between her highly groomed appearance and the blue-collar setting. But, in general, I think we know full well why some people's appearance receives more attention than others: absence of the Y chromosome. For instance, I Googled the phrase 'Hillary Clinton dressed' and returned 1,170 pages. 'Barack Obama dressed' returned only 167, many of those about a caricature of him wearing a turban and robes. Time and again reporters will mention what a woman is wearing, even though they would not do the same if the person in question were a man in the same capacity.

Many people, including many women, neither notice this nor care much about it if it is pointed out. Perhaps, they'll say, it's just that men tend to look very similar – all in suits and ties – whereas women provide more aesthetic variety, for which they are noticed. There may be something in that. But there is surely also something in the complaint that to describe what a woman is wearing when it is irrelevant to the story in hand has the subtle effect of slightly undermining the seriousness of the woman in question. By placing some importance on how she looks, you take away some of the importance of what she says.

There are many other ways in which women are treated or talked about differently from men. Young women, for example, are often described as 'girls' when men of the same age are not called 'boys'. Strength in women is also more likely to be linked with negative attributes such as 'coldness' than strength in men, which is almost always seen as a good thing.

It is easy to dismiss concerns about this as attempts to make mountains out of molehills. But perhaps a better analogy is with heaps of sand. Each small instance, like a single grain of sand, is indeed insignificant by itself. But the cumulative effect of thousands of such reinforcements of stereotypes adds up, just as enough grains of sand will fill a desert. And that there are millions of such grains is indisputable. Just consider the William

James quote I opened with. He talked not of a person's self but a 'man's self'. If the male is made the paradigm of the human, the female is inevitably relegated to second place.

Arguments that small differences in language and behaviour subtly undermine certain social groups seem to be finding fewer, not more, supporters by the day. One reason is a justified suspicion of an argument which rests on the accumulation of imperceptible biases. You might well ask, how would we know if it is indeed the case that small differences in the use of language have such big effects? How can I be so sure that commenting on a woman's clothes really subtly suggests the things I claim it does? Even if you suspect I'm right, can't this same kind of argument be used to support less feasible claims? Should we go so far as to avoid talking about black sheep, black markets and blackmail because it subtly reinforces the sense that being black is bad?

See also

14. The wonder of colourpuncture

Loading the dice

Julie (she's open to spiritual stuff) and Kate (the cynical one) continue their voyage of discovery through the world of the New Age. This month our testing twosome try colourpuncture.

Spirit and Destiny[20]

Imagine you're a comedy writer and you want to send up New Age, alternative medicine. 'Colourpuncture' would be a stroke of comedic genius. But too late – it's already out there, and it's for real.

According to *Spirit and Destiny* magazine, colourpuncture was devised by a German scientist who 'discovered that there was a connection between the network of Chinese meridians in our bodies and the healing effect of light-responsive colours'. Well, I can see one obvious connection – neither really exists.

To call *Spirit and Destiny* flaky would be an insult to flakes. The only problem with identifying a bad argument in it is to know where to begin. The extract I've selected contains a good example of 'loading the dice'. This is when something is presented as if it were mere description when in fact it contains one or more implied value judgements.

So, you notice that Julie is described as 'open', which is generally considered to be a good thing. This in itself implies that her counterpart, Kate, has a closed mind, which is not something to be proud of. It gets worse for Kate, however. She is not described as sceptical but 'cynical'. Whereas 'open' implies an unbiased, impartial attitude, 'cynical' suggests prejudice against the spiritual.

So when Julie and Kate set about 'testing' colourpuncture, the dice has been loaded. Were Kate to report negatively, we would be able to dismiss her views as those of a closed-minded sceptic. We can trust Julie, on the other hand, if she gives a favourable verdict, since she's open-minded and fair. And what's more, theirs is a 'voyage of discovery', implying at the outset that what is being 'tested' is a wonderful world of wisdom and knowledge, not a dubious sea of sloppy-minded rubbish.

As it happens, Kate ends up scoring colourpuncture even more highly than Julie! It must be impressive to have persuaded such an old cynic as her. Not that her scepticism seems particularly hard-nosed. She is easily impressed by the therapist's own leaflet which claims 'The effects are so well proven, that German insurance companies will fund treatments.' 'Cynical' Kate doesn't even raise an eyebrow. Instead, she swoons, 'Ahh, insurer backing and Teutonic endorsement, that's the kind of logic I like.'

It looks probable, then, that the dice has been loaded in more ways than one here. Loading by language is perhaps the least obvious. It's something that can happen a lot without us noticing. For example, cross-pollination of genetically modified and non-genetically modified crops is referred to by environmentalists as 'genetic pollution'. Since 'pollution' clearly has negative connotations, this description makes the cross-pollination sound bad before any argument or evidence is presented that it is bad.

The problem seems clear enough. But is it always possible to throw a fair dice? Sometimes it seems that describing something in value-free language is either not possible or ridiculously euphemistic. Often, the best we can do is choose our words carefully, try not to load the dice and be aware of the implied judgements in the words we read and write. I'm sure that intelligent, open readers will agree with me, but am prepared to take criticism from cynical or slow ones. That's only fair, after all.

It's not difficult to find examples of where loading the dice in some way or another seems unavoidable. For example, in the Iraqi conflict, such words as 'liberation' and 'occupation' carry evaluative connotations. But is it possible to describe what happened there without resorting to language which carries some hint of judgement? An even trickier example is that of clitoridectomy. This clinical term is far too formal and obscure for most contexts, but should it be glossed as 'female genital cutting' or as 'female genital mutilation'? The latter clearly implies a strong moral disapproval, but is anything else just over-sensitive avoidance of the truth?

See also

15. Who knows?

Arguments from uncertainty

> This textbook discusses evolution, a controversial theory
> some scientists present as a scientific explanation for the
> origin of living things, such as plants, animals and humans.
> No one was present when life first appeared on earth.
> Therefore, any statement about life's origins should be
> considered as theory, not fact.
>
> Notice put in all biology textbooks by the Alabama State Board
> of Education, 1996–2001

The teaching of evolution in American schools has always
been controversial. In the 1925 'Scopes Monkey Trial', a
Tennessee teacher was found guilty of teaching evolution in
contravention of a state law known as the Butler Act, which
was repealed only in 1967. The following year, the Supreme
Court ruled that a similar law in Arkansas violated the First
Amendment. In 2005, the US District Court for the Middle
District of Pennsylvania ruled that Intelligent Design did not
belong on the science curriculum. Similar controversies still
rumble on.

Most scientists despair in the face of this, unable to understand why so many resist the theory of evolution when the
scientific evidence for its truth is so overwhelming. But resist
people do, and not just in America. A poll conducted for the

BBC's *Horizon* programme found that just 48 per cent of Britons believed evolution best described their view of the origin and development of life; 22 per cent preferred creationism and 17 per cent Intelligent Design.[21]

There are many reasons why evolution is hard to swallow, and one is surely that people are too impressed by the claim that evolution is 'theory, not fact'.

Evolution is indeed a theory. We also do not know for certain that it is true. But this in itself is an uninteresting claim. Arguably, we know nothing for certain. Maybe we are not hominids walking the earth at all, but lizards plugged into a virtual reality machine on Alpha Centauri, fed the illusion of normal terrestrial life. This is highly unlikely, but it's possible and we don't know for absolute certain that we are not being deceived in this or in countless other fanciful ways.

If we taught in our schools only facts known with complete certainty, we would teach nothing at all. What we do instead is teach things which we have overwhelming evidence to believe are the case. What we call 'facts' are not iron-clad certainties, but beliefs which admit of no reasonable doubt or are overwhelmingly probable.

The Alabama State Board of Education, however, wanted to make too much of the uncertainty surrounding evolution. It could have done this in an intellectually respectable way, by claiming that the theory is too uncertain to be taught without alternatives being offered, such as creationism or Intelligent Design. This way of teaching is not unprecedented: history teachers, for example, are always making their students aware of competing versions of what really happened.

The claim would not stand up, however, because almost all scientists agree that the evidence for evolution is as strong as the evidence for countless other uncontroversial scientific hypotheses. While there are uncertainties as to exactly how evolution works, the claim that life has evolved on Earth is as certain as any scientific claim can be.

So instead the board decided simply to appeal to the fact/theory distinction as though that clinched it, while making additional claims about the theory being 'controversial', which it is among the general public but not at all among those who really understand it. Scientific controversy surrounds the details of how evolution works, not whether it does.

People seem to think that uncertainty always demands shoulder-shrugging. In fact, certitude is a matter of degree. Where there is less of it, you don't always need to suspend judgement. It is often enough merely to remain open to the unlikely but possible discovery that you are wrong. Good thinking requires neither making too much of the inherent uncertainty of our beliefs nor settling into a false sense of security.

The mere presence of uncertainty may not demand agnosticism. But when do things become so unclear that suspension of judgement really is the best choice? Should one be an agnostic because God's non-existence is not certain? Should you have no opinion on whether there is life after death, since by definition no one can know for sure what will happen to them when their heart packs up? Should we dismiss the 9/11 Commission's report because its findings might be wrong? How certain are you that uncertainty is sufficient grounds for suspending belief?

See also

16. My luck's got to change

The gambler's fallacy

He's due a win.

Damon Hack, *New York Times*[22]

When people say they are 'due a win', in sport, gambling or, more metaphorically, in life in general, they are more often than not doing little more than expressing a hope born of despair. But sometimes they also believe that in a very literal sense their luck is due to change.

The idea, usually vaguely rather than explicitly held, is that nature balances things up in the long run, so a recent series of results going one way requires a balancing set of results going the other. Otherwise, the world is out of joint.

Perhaps the clearest evidence that many people do think like this is the popularity of websites that tell you how many times numbers have been picked in national and state lotteries. The fact that people consult these sites makes sense only if they believe that past selections can provide some kind of indicator of the likelihood of future ones.

Sometimes people believe this for superstitious reasons, but on other occasions they are making a mistake about the probability of random occurrences known as 'the gambler's fallacy'. Take the toss of a fair coin. The chances of it coming up heads or tails is 50–50. That means that if you toss it 100 times, it is likely to come up heads about as often as it will come up tails. But this does not mean it is likely that you'll get exactly fifty heads and fifty tails. Each toss of the coin is a distinct event and does not affect the tosses that follow or precede it: if fifty tails have already been tossed, nature does not 'know' that a head is due, or vice versa.

Another source of the mistake is a misapprehension of the nature of unlikely events. For example, the chance of tossing ten heads in a row is one in 1,024. Let us say that we have tossed a coin nine times in a row and it has come up heads every time. Surely, people feel, since the chances of a series of ten is so unlikely, it must be more likely that the next toss is tails rather than heads? Wrong. The unlikely (one in 512 chance) sequence of nine heads prior to this toss does not affect the outcome of the tenth toss. What is really unlikely has already happened. The probability that a tenth head will be tossed from this starting point is thus not one in 1,024 but 50–50, because it hinges on one toss which, like all the others, is an evens bet.

Although it is a straightforward fallacy to suppose past random events affect the outcome of future ones, you might nonetheless justifiably see an unlikely series as being evidence that the sequence isn't random at all. For example, if a coin has been tossed heads nine times in a row, you might bet on heads for the tenth on the basis that you suspect the tossing isn't random. That's perfectly reasonable, just as long as you understand that the mere occurrence of the unlikely series does not in itself show that the tossing has not been fair. It is of the nature of unlikely events that they will occasionally happen.

Pundits are keen on the 'due a win' trope. Damon Hack used it when tipping Retief Goosen to win the 2006 golf Open. Bobby Clampett of Turner Sports also decreed that the

Europeans were due a victory in the tournament. As it turned out, Goosen finished fourteenth, eleven shots behind the winner, the American Tiger Woods. To be fair to both, however, golf is one of the more unpredictable sports, and in this context the phrase 'due a win' is not always an example of the gambler's fallacy at all, but simply an expression of the belief that a team or player is playing so well they are likely to win sooner or later. When you next hear someone say that an occurrence is due, ask yourself why before assuming they're guilty of fallacious thinking.

Here's a question you can pose to yourself and others to see how much in the grip of the fallacy you are. Jack and Jim are betting on Frida's toss of a fair coin, twenty times in a row. Jack thinks that the result of the previous tosses influences the result of the toss that follows. Jim, having read about the gambler's fallacy, knows that this is not true. Who is more likely to win more of the bets, Jack or Jim?

Answer on page 315

See also

17. If you won't kill it don't eat it

Won't and shouldn't

If ministers had to accompany the troops, we would be back home by Monday week.

Martin Samuel, *The Times*[23]

Confucius's golden rule was 'Do not do to others that which you do not want done to you.' The golden rule for many pacifists and vegetarians seems to be 'Do not have done to others that which you would not do to them yourself.'

It's an extremely popular moral maxim. Anti-war campaigners berate hawks on the grounds that they usually show little willingness to get out on the battlefield and face the enemy themselves. Opponents of capital punishment can make those with the contrary view squirm by asking if they would be prepared to deliver the fatal injection themselves. Anti-abortionists use images of terminated foetuses to suggest that we can maintain support for abortion only if we keep ourselves far removed from the act itself. The message of them all is that if you can't do it yourself, then you're a hypocrite to say it's all right for others to do it on your behalf.

The undeniable rhetorical force of the argument is not, however, supported by any rational argument. There is no necessary link between the rightness or wrongness of an action and one's ability or inability to do it. This can easily be seen by considering all four possible connections that could be claimed between approval or disapproval and the willingness or unwillingness to act:

1. If someone is willing to perform an action, that action is wrong
2. If someone is willing to perform an action, that action is right
3. If someone is unwilling to perform an action, that action is right
4. If someone is unwilling to perform an action, that action is wrong

The first and third of these are obvious nonsense. The second is also clearly false. Anti-abortionists see people who are willing to carry out the terminations as wicked, not as a challenge to their values. Doves think the same of gun-toting hawks, as do opponents of capital punishment of those willing to act as executioner. All this would be surprising if one's willingness to carry out an action were any kind of indicator of its moral status.

Which leaves the original case, fourth on the list, where an unwillingness to perform an action is supposed to indicate that there is something morally suspect about it. Yet the only thing that follows from such an inability is the psychological truth that we are disinclined to do what we find unpleasant. But since when has unpleasantness been any kind of reliable moral barometer? Most people would recoil from performing an autopsy, yet that doesn't make autopsies immoral. Many of us would find it too unpleasant to kill someone or put our lives at great risk in a heroic act to save others, yet that says something only about us, not about the morality of what we cannot do. Since the fact that we are unwilling or unable to do something does not make it wrong, there is nothing hypocritical about both believing something is right and not having the stomach to do it oneself.

Indeed, it is often the mark of acts of great moral bravery that ordinary people recoil from them. But you don't hear people saying 'I think that if you are not prepared to attempt air-sea rescue yourself, you ought not to take advantage of it if it's offered to you,' or 'I can't stand these people who support helping the poor in third world countries but who aren't prepared to get out there and do it themselves.' In these examples, the absurdity is apparent. But the logic is exactly the same as in the previous cases of vegetarianism, capital punishment and war: an inability or unwillingness to do something yourself is taken to be a sign that you ought not to approve of it.

I suspect that the reason why the move is so popular is that it is reasonable to ask people in some way to confront the reality of what they support, if that reality is unpleasant. Asking someone to imagine actually doing what it is they support is thus a way of focusing minds on what is at stake. It is an aid to moral deliberation, not a short-cut to a conclusion.

Are there any unpleasant implications of what you believe which you are unwilling or unable to face up to? If you support capital punishment, do you fully realize that it results in the death of a human being, sometimes the wrong one? If you are a carnivore, or simply drink milk, do you shirk from the reality that animals must die so you can get your meat or dairy products? If you are pro-choice, do you realize just what is being destroyed in an abortion? Your emotional reactions to these thoughts may not sound moral intuitions, but don't they tell you at least something? If so, what?

See also

18. Fast food made me obese

Shifting agency

> Seventeen estates will get cash this year. That's just a fraction of the 3,000 deprived neighbourhoods where children like Amy, Hayley, John and Stephen are being denied the opportunities most of us expect.
>
> Kim Catcheside, BBC social affairs correspondent[24]

Linguists are as useful as logicians when it comes to spotting rhetorical sleights of hand. A small difference in sentence construction can significantly alter the import of an utterance.

One of the most important things language can do is convey information about agency: who did what. Even small children seem to realize instinctively the opportunities this presents to put a more neutral spin on otherwise incriminating information: why say 'I broke the toy' when you could say 'The toy broke'?

We can use all sorts of alternative constructions to shift the perceived agent of an action or event. For instance, 'I feel humiliated' is a neutral description of our own emotional state, whereas 'You humiliated me' firmly identifies the cause of that feeling with another person. But the latter could be misleading, if it is the case that your feelings of humiliation are mainly the result of your own insecurity or sensitivity rather than of malicious or thoughtless actions by others.

Kim Catcheside used a similarly dubious way of putting things in a BBC news item about special funding for deprived neighbourhoods. She quite rightly wanted to end her report by pointing out that, for all the fine words about what the new government money would do, it wouldn't change the lives of the vast majority of those who live in such areas. But she described the plight of these people in an odd way: she said they 'are being denied the opportunities most of us expect'. Had she said that they 'don't have' these opportunities, her comment would have been neutral as to who is responsible for this, or indeed if anyone is responsible at all. But by saying they 'are being denied', there was a clear implication that someone is actively withholding opportunities from them. A sense of agency was introduced, and with it a sense of responsibility.

You may think this is right, but clearly such a view of the situation is a politically loaded one and you would not expect an impartial BBC report to introduce such a viewpoint. Nor is it the case that no neutral descriptions were available.

Of course, it is possible to read the sentence in more abstract terms, so that the children in question were 'being denied' by no more than fate or chance. That may be all that was meant, but the implication of agency is not just some optional extra, or over-zealous interpretation: it's there in the grammar. If we don't intend to imply a responsible agent, we should not use constructions which do just that.

Likewise, if there was a responsible agent, we should not cover up the fact. There is a phrase which is used quite a lot these days which does just this: 'It didn't happen.' We might talk enthusiastically about arranging a get-together of old friends for a weekend but never get round to it. Someone may ask us, 'Whatever came of that weekend you were planning?' 'It didn't happen,' we reply, as though the failure of the event to occur had nothing to do with our own disorganization. Although social events don't *just happen*, it seems they can *just not happen* of their own accord.

Implications of agency are deeply imbedded in our language: we should therefore pick out words carefully if we want to be accurate about who caused what.

How accurate or misleading are the following, frequently heard, statements? 'We found ourselves at a strip club,' 'She led me on,' 'Ten civilians died during the air raid,' 'Fast food made me obese,' 'This book has taught me nothing.' There are different ways of expressing the same things: would they be more or less accurate?

See also

19. If it ain't clear, it ain't real

Real and fuzzy distinctions

> I was calling the life inside me a baby because I wanted it.
> Yet if I hadn't, I would think of it just as a group of cells that
> it was OK to kill. It was the same entity. It was merely my
> response to it that determined whether it would live or
> die. That seemed irrational to me. Maybe even immoral.

Miranda Sawyer, *Observer*[25]

It is a common complaint that life is full of grey areas, yet
people prefer to think in black and white. Oddly, however, this
remark is often directed at advocates of reason and logic, as
though it was the desire to think as clearly as possible which
leads people to forget this simple truth. Although there are
examples of philosophers who have tried to cleave conceptual
distinctions more cleanly than nature permits, good thinking
should help, not hinder, our journey through life's foggier areas.

The journalist Miranda Sawyer, for instance, seemed to be
shrouded in some kind of cognitive mist when she thought
about her own response to the positive result of a pregnancy test.
Writing about how having a child changed her views on abortion,
Sawyer stated that she now felt troubled, when previously she
had been unambiguously pro-choice. At the core of her worries
was a typical concern about what exactly is inside the womb of
the expectant mother. Is it just a collection of cells or is it a human

baby? Sawyer thought there was no answer to that: it was whatever we chose to call it. But that was disturbing, because it suggested that the difference between killing a child and killing a few cells is a matter of semantics.

The obvious reply is that what at conception starts out as a collection of cells gradually becomes a human baby. But the trouble with this is that any cut-off point would seem to be arbitrary. No wonder anti-abortionists try to clear up this unsatisfactory vagueness by insisting it is always a child, right from conception.

Both these 'pro-lifers' and Sawyer seem to me to be making a basic mistake, which is to think that unless there is a firm boundary between two states or concepts, there is no real distinction between them, and the best we can do is make one up. Applying it to the case of proto-human cells and babies, Sawyer concludes that the lack of a meaningful distinction leaves us in moral confusion, while anti-abortionists say that such a meaningless distinction has to be dropped and replaced by the single category of human life from conception.

Whatever the ethics of abortion, the reasoning behind both these positions is deeply flawed. Language and logic may have a problem describing fuzzy boundaries in nature, but it should be obvious both that such boundaries exist and that distinctions they cleave are real nonetheless. Colour is a clear example. Arrange all the colours along a spectrum and you will find no determinate point at which red becomes orange, or green blue. Yet there is a clear and important distinction between orange and red, green and blue. This is the case even though one cannot draw a clear line between them.

Likewise, those who claim there is a real distinction between cells that are not yet a person and a fully formed human are in no way refuted by the observation that they are unable to say at which point one becomes the other. The absence of a clear, determinate boundary is no argument against the existence of a real distinction.

Clear thinking hence helps us to understand the nature of life's grey areas; it does not deny them. Resistance to ambiguity tends to be more psychological than logical. For instance, it is sometimes hard to know whether to describe an armed militia as terrorists or freedom fighters. Rather than try to live with the uncertainty, it is tempting to deny the meaningfulness of the distinction. However, that simply suits both the authorities who want to brand all resistance groups as terrorists, and terrorists who want to claim moral parity with freedom fighters.

How easy do you find it to maintain a distinction without drawing a line? Do you accept a difference between legitimate business and ruthless capitalism? Constructive charity and destructive pity? Justified armed intervention and illegal, immoral military aggression? Legitimate sexual experimentation and harmful perversion?

See also

20. Radiohead changed my life

It worked for me . . .

> It would be interesting to see how the world would be
> different if Dick Cheney really listened to Radiohead's *OK
> Computer*. I think the world would probably improve. That
> album is fucking brilliant. It changed my life, so why
> wouldn't it change his?

Chris Martin of Coldplay[26]

Our ability to predict what will happen and to detect order in
the world depends upon a type of argument which is strictly
speaking illogical. Induction is a form of reasoning which allows
us to infer general principles from particular experiences.
Sometimes we have many particulars to work on: countless
observations have shown water to be H_2O, so the hypothesis
that all water is so composed seems pretty secure. However, we
often generalize on the basis of very few observations. If you
have a new gadget, you press a button and something happens,
and you assume the same thing will happen if you press the
button again. This is because your reasoning is informed by
many other similar experiences which create a general assumption about regularity in the function of buttons. But whether we
base our generalizations on many instances or just one or two,
we are still concluding that something is always the case on the
basis of only a limited set of observations.

Even setting these theoretical worries aside, in practice the temptation to over-generalize on the basis of a potentially misleading particular experience can be almost irresistible. Chris Martin's comments about Dick Cheney and Radiohead are an especially egregious example of the mistake. It is hard to believe that Martin really thinks listening to an album which is lyrically opaque and nothing like a coherent political treatise would change the mind of someone who has spent their whole life developing a political outlook. But 'It changed my life, so why wouldn't it change his?'

What Martin has ignored is that people's reactions to music and art are extremely variable. So the fact that *OK Computer* changed his life is no guarantee at all that it will change the lives of others. In fact, the evidence that it often won't is staring him in the face, since Martin must know full well that some people hate that album.

When people over-generalize from a limited number of specific instances they are said to be reading too much into merely 'anecdotal evidence'. But this phrase is a little misleading, since sometimes one or two instances are enough to form at least a tentative general hypothesis. It is not strictly the number of cases you base your reasoning on that counts, but whether they are of the right kind.

It may be hard to specify precisely what the right kind is, but the typical features of the wrong kind are clear enough. As in the example of Martin, you cannot generalize from situations where there are known to be considerable variations in how people or things respond.

But there is another problem with Martin's generalization which is more typical of arguments from anecdotal evidence: an assumption that the cases they generalize from actually have the characteristics they think they do. Did *OK Computer* really change Martin's life? Perhaps, but I am pretty sure it didn't change him from a Cheneyite neo-con to an anti-capitalist. So it is not just that the album wouldn't have the effect claimed for it on all people; it didn't even have that effect on Martin.

Chris Martin's hyperbole notwithstanding, personal recommendations are often the most satisfying to follow up. Nevertheless, I'm sure you too have had the experience of doing something that someone has recommended with such conviction you were sure there must be something in it, only to find it was not your cup of tea at all. How then to share your experiences and enthusiasm with others without misleading them? My personal ploy is to try to think of reasons why others might not like something I do, and at least flag these up. You might want to try it, but I should warn you it does have drawbacks: some will see your measured approach as betraying doubts rather than careful thought. Consideration weighs, but conviction sways.

See also

21. Mood music

The power of suggestion

Are you thinking what we're thinking?

UK Conservative Party 2005 election manifesto slogan

Elections are a sobering time for people who like to think that arguments count and that opinions can be shifted by rational debate. Sound arguments have little to do with the success or failure of campaigns. What seems to matter most is the overall impression given by the various candidates. This is why all the main parties are quite justifiably very concerned with image.

When a political party is making its case by, in effect, not really making a case at all but creating an impression, it can be hard to pinpoint errors of reasoning. Indeed, a really good campaign will use vacuous platitudes which are irrefutable, as was the case with the British Conservatives in 2005. Consider some of their slogans: 'What's wrong with a little discipline in schools?' Why, nothing of course. 'It's not racist to impose limits on immigration.' Of course it isn't. 'Why can't politicians be more accountable?' Good question!

The election was fought using slogans that were on the whole correct. Where the sleight of hand occurred is that, when such words and slogans are selected and put together in the right way, an overall impression is created which is distinct from that of the individual elements themselves. Each utterance, each slogan, is a single note which helps create the 'mood music' only if it is played in the right place at the right time.

Several of the motifs for the Conservative campaign's mood music were very clear and catchy. One theme was fear. Speaking at the launch of his party's Welsh manifesto, Conservative leader Michael Howard said, 'I want criminals to look over their shoulders in fear – not the law-abiding public. And I use that word deliberately – fear.' This was clever stuff. Howard was talking about making criminals afraid of being caught, and who could be against that? But fear is a theme he kept returning to, and it is hard to avoid concluding that the real aim was to keep hitting that note so as to create a climate of insecurity among the electorate, and the impression that the Conservatives were the ones who would reduce it.

So it was with talk of immigration controls, unruly schoolchildren and dirty hospitals. Cumulatively, the impression given was that we should be afraid, very afraid, especially of people who are different, such as gypsies and asylum seekers. Yet individually, the statements on all these issues were innocuous. 'It's not racist to impose limits on immigration.' True.

I've focused on the 2005 Conservative campaign, but all the political parties now play the same game. They are utilizing what I believe is one of the most powerful rhetorical tricks available, precisely because it cannot be pinned down to errors in logic or dodgy inferences. It is hard even to establish that it has been made. Because this is all about impressions created, not statements made, it can be claimed that anyone who interprets the mood music unfavourably has simply got the wrong impression. My perceptions, it will be argued, reflect only my prejudices.

However, it is no secret that the Conservatives were using the so–called 'dog whistle' technique: saying things that deliver messages only the intended audience can hear. Since this whole strategy relies on there being implicit as well as explicit messages, the claim that some things are being implied which are not actually being said can hardly be denied. The room for dis-agreement concerns only what those implied messages are.

As marketing gets increasingly sophisticated, such 'dog whistles' are being blown all the time. Look and listen carefully, however, and you may just be able to pick them up.

How many of the products you buy have you purchased because you have sound reason to think they are better? Can you honestly say you haven't been swayed by the overall impression the mar-keting people have carefully cultivated? Take a look around your house, in your food cupboards, in your wardrobe and even at your car. How much have you been moving to the beat of the marke-teer's mood music?

See also

22. Careful with your Johnson!

Insensitivity to context

> Why, Sir, you find no man at all intellectual who is willing to leave London: No, Sir, when a man is tired of London, he is tired of life; for there is in London all that life can afford.
>
> Samuel Johnson[27]

Dr Johnson's paean to London is oft-repeated as if it were an established truth: to admit to being fed up with Britain's capital is to admit to being worn out with life itself. But even if what Johnson claimed were true, that still leaves several problems for those who would appeal to its truth to support their love of modern-day London. The most obvious of these is that the observation is 200 years out of date. In 1801, ten years after the publication of Boswell's *Life of Samuel Johnson*, London's population was 900,000. In 2002 it was 7.4 million. But for the existence of many historic buildings, Johnson wouldn't even recognize the London of today, let alone be in any position to judge whether it was the best place in the world to live.

Furthermore, a cursory examination of the context of Johnson's quote shows that it doesn't even express a general approval of London life at all. Johnson is talking only of the lives of 'intellectual' men. Of course, an intellectual at that time would mean a member of the comfortable middle classes, and most definitely a man rather than a woman. People outside this exclusive circle, intelligent or otherwise, could understandably be tired of London not out of tiredness with life but out of a hunger to live a better one.

Consider this description by Richard Schwartz in his *Daily Life in Johnson's London*. 'Hovels and shacks were commonplace. Many of the poor crowded into deserted houses. A sizeable number of the city's inhabitants both lived and worked below ground level.'[28] Even in Johnson's time, there were plenty of good reasons to tire of London.

In this case the insensitivity to context is usually unobjectionable. Quotations take on a life of their own and can be used simply to express a sentiment in a particularly pithy way. I myself have used Yeats's 'The best lack all conviction, while the worst are full of passionate intensity' out of context to celebrate the lack of conviction Yeats is actually lamenting in the original poem. (I've also misattributed it, which is less forgivable.) In a similar way, when people trot out Johnson's line they are usually doing no more than borrowing some words to express how they feel better than they could using their own words. However, if we are taking something as authoritative, to *justify* as well as to *express* what we think, then ignoring context is inexcusable.

Another striking example of this kind of contextual insensitivity is Marx and Engels's claim, made in the *Communist Manifesto* in 1848 that 'The proletarians have nothing to lose but their chains.' Even the proudest unreconstructed Marxist would have to admit, given the huge differences between the conditions of the working classes today and 150 years ago, that if this assertion is still true it needs to be shown to be still true. One cannot pretend that a claim made at a particular historical time and place becomes timelessly true simply in virtue of being repeated enough over the years.

Most of us have favourite quotes we like to brandish around to justify as well as express our beliefs, but when was the last time you went back to the source and checked what the author really meant? Try it: you might find that ideas you thought were clear and settled are actually less straightforward and more interesting.

See also

23. The end is nigh (perhaps)

Concealed caveats

Now the Pentagon tells Bush: climate change will destroy us.

Observer headline[29]

In Britain at least, we expect newspaper headlines to overstate their case a little. But in this particular example from 2004, the story turned out to be just as dramatic as the headline suggested. Apparently, a Pentagon report 'warns that major European cities will be sunk beneath rising seas as Britain is plunged into a "Siberian" climate by 2020'.

In a box accompanying the article headed 'The key findings', we also discovered that 'by 2007 violent storms smash coastal barriers rendering large parts of the Netherlands uninhabitable. Cities like The Hague are abandoned.'

Well, 2007 has been and gone and The Hague is still there. So what went wrong at the Pentagon? Nothing: these were never firm predictions at all. Rather, they were just some of the more extreme scenarios that it was thought could happen as a result of global warming. All the caveats were suppressed so as to be virtually invisible.

The article should have used predominantly conditional forms – such as 'may', 'could' and 'might' – along with some indication of how probable these outcomes were considered to be. But instead, it was largely written in the future tense – 'Nuclear conflict, mega-droughts, famine and widespread rioting will erupt across the world' – or in the present simple – 'riots and internal conflict tear apart India and Indonesia.' Phrased in this way, the events described seem to be firm predictions, not merely possibilities among many.

There were a few 'coulds' scattered about, but definite indicative verb forms vastly outnumbered these. Indeed, you needed to look carefully to be sure that the report in question dealt only with possibilities and not firm predictions. The clearest evidence that this was the case came in the comment that, according to the report, 'an imminent scenario of catastrophic climate change is "plausible".' To say these outcomes were plausible is very different to saying they were predicted – a word used elsewhere in the article – or even probable. And it is certainly misleading to describe as 'findings' scenarios that are no more than plausible.

This article was an extreme example, but subtler failures to include the caveats and qualifications that are required to make what is said accurate are all too common.

Sometimes, it is arguable whether or not the lack of a qualification is a failure or merely a case of acceptable stylistic economy, since the caveat can be safely assumed. For example, an article in the *Guardian* included the sentence, 'Mynak Tulku, the reincarnation of a powerful lama, is the Dragon King's unofficial ambassador for new technology.'[30] It would have been more accurate to have written something like 'believed to be the reincarnation of a powerful lama'. But arguably such caveats can be assumed: we all know that whether he is in fact reincarnated is a matter of opinion. In the context of this particular article, I think the lack of caveat contributes to an unquestioning acceptance of the beliefs of Bhutan's Buddhists, but this could be seen as quibbling.

Between the borderline case of the reincarnated lama and the extreme case of global catastrophe starting next year lie many instances where caveats are either missing entirely or played down. As writers, we need to make sure we include all the caveats that are necessary to make what we say true and which we cannot assume the reader will take for granted. And as readers, we need to be aware that many writers are not as vigilant as this, and look out for the signs of concealed or absent qualifications.

'Spot the caveats' is a game you can play reading any newspaper or watching any news bulletin. All you need to do is look out for striking claims, usually in the headlines, and then see how long it takes for someone to reveal the qualifications that make them less striking after all. If no one does, go online to try to find them. If you still can't find them, congratulations! You've found a rare example of a genuinely amazing story. Play just a few times and you realize just how hyped most news stories are.

No prizes for spotting such failures in this book, but you might enjoy looking, especially if you succeed in finding some.

See also

24. Good for the goose, good for the gander

Tu quoque

> The onnagata [male actors in the kabuki theatre who play female roles] justify their perpetual monopoly by saying they believe that women are too close to femininity to capture its essence.
>
> Richard Eyre, theatre and film director[31]

Looking back at the rationales the dominant classes used to offer to justify their oppression of others, it is remarkable how paper-thin their arguments often were. Unless we are prepared to say that people were simply more stupid back then, the most likely explanation as to why these arguments washed is that the reasons people give to support their beliefs often have very little to do with the real reasons why they hold them. It also seems that we are good at convincing ourselves of the rationality of the most irrational of prejudices.

The reasoning of the onnagata is a striking example of privilege being given a pseudo-rational gloss. Their justification for excluding women from the kabuki theatre, if true, would seem also to entail that men should not portray men. Consistency would seem to demand that men played women and women played men, not that men should play all roles.

This objection is of the general type 'tu quoque': you too. It identifies any number of bad argumentative moves by showing that they make a criticism or objection which applies equally to the person making it. In this case, the reason the onnagata give against women playing women applies equally to men playing men.

However, there are two reasons why this move is not quite as obviously powerful as it might initially seem. First, very often the alleged lack of consistency on which the move depends may require some establishing. In the case of the onnagata, for example, it is arguable that I haven't yet shown that the principle can in fact be decisively turned against them. I have not, for example, considered the possibility that the onnagata have some good reasons for thinking that women are closer to femininity than men are to masculinity. If that were the case (and I admit, it is hard to see how it could be), there would indeed be a reason why women shouldn't play women which doesn't apply to men playing men.

Nonetheless, the *tu quoque* move does at least force us to confront the apparent inconsistency. The onnagata, if they are at all interested in defending their practices rationally, would either have to accept the inconsistency or explain why it is not an inconsistency after all. Either way, we are taken closer to the heart of the issue.

The second problem with *tu quoque* is that it is not a means of identifying which principles and arguments are actually wrong. Let us say, for example, that we are satisfied that the onnagata are guilty of inconsistency. Does that mean that they are wrong to say that women are too close to femininity to capture its essence; or does it simply mean that they are right, but that they should also accept that men are too close to masculinity to capture its essence?

The choice is between giving up the principle that leads to the inconsistency or holding on to it and accepting other principles that remove the inconsistency. Nothing about *tu quoque* tells us which option is more rational.

The next time you turn a criticism back at your criticizer, ask yourself whether both or neither of you should be uncomfortable. For example, if you are told your car is emitting too much CO_2 and you reply that your accuser also emits as much CO_2 on their annual holiday flight, does that get you off the hook or merely show that your accuser needs to change too? Just because other people aren't always as honest as they should be, does that excuse our own dissembling? And if we ourselves are found guilty of constructing bad arguments, does that make the poor reasoning of others any less incorrect?

See also

25. One, two, three, four, we don't want your fascist war!

Fallacies of democracy

> Although the majority of the public were always against the war, this was not reflected by their elected representatives. The government behaved in a way that was transparently undemocratic . . .
>
> Brian Eno, musician[32]

In 2003, the musician Damon Albarn complained about the seemingly inexorable movement of the UK government towards war in Iraq, saying, 'I don't think we have been consulted as a democracy.'[33] The war went ahead anyway. Looking back in 2007, Brian Eno made much the same complaint. Call me a cynic, but when two rock singers are in agreement, I suspect something is wrong.

But weren't Albarn and Eno right? During the build-up to the invasion of Iraq, opinion polls showed a majority of people against going to war with Iraq. So isn't it true that to start a war in defiance of the wishes of the British people was profoundly undemocratic?

This argument is flawed in several respects. Presumably, it is not premised on the 'democratic fallacy': the view that majority opinion is always right. It would be absurd to think that beliefs become true or false on the basis of how many people hold them.

This crude fallacy is obviously not what most people have in mind when they claim Britain's involvement in the second Iraq war was undemocratic. However, simply acknowledging that public opinion can be wrong immediately exposes the weakness of other arguments that war was an affront against democracy.

For instance, one can accept that the majority can be wrong but insist that, nevertheless, in a democracy majority opinion must be followed, for better or for worse. But this confuses democracy with simple majoritarianism. Democracy is a system of government in which the supreme power is vested in the people but is exercised through a system of representation. A crude majoritarian system, in contrast, is one where the government always does what the majority wants.

Most democracies are not majoritarian. If Britain were run on majoritarian lines, for example, then fox-hunting would have been banned long ago and capital punishment would never have been abolished. In other words, Britain would be a country which killed more people but fewer animals.

Majoritarianism is not the favoured system in the West, partly to protect minorities, and partly because majorities are often wrong. Britain, like other Western nations, runs on the model of a representative democracy. In this system, members of parliament are elected as representatives to make decisions on behalf of their electors, not as delegates to do whatever their electors tell them. They are held to account every four to five years at elections, when they are judged on their overall record.

It therefore cannot be said to be undemocratic for parliament to act against the wishes of the majority of the population at any given time. This very possibility is just what distinguishes representative democracies from majoritarian regimes. The British parliament, elected by the people, made a decision to go to war and members of that parliament will be re-elected or voted out by the people at the next election. That is paradigmatically democratic.

Public opinion is, in any case, hardly settled. In February 2003 an ICM poll showed that only 29 per cent of the British public supported a war on Iraq. By mid-April, following the fall of Baghdad, support had risen to 63 per cent. YouGov's tracker poll shows that support for the war was greater than opposition to it until November. Opposition to the war became the settled verdict of the people only after May 2004. Arguably, this shows how the fickleness of public opinion is another good reason why genuinely democratic governments cannot and should not always follow it.

All this raises very profound questions about the nature of democracy. If we accept, as surely we must, that democracy is not just about doing whatever the people want at any given time, what is the appropriate link between the decisions of politicians and the general will? Elections may give people the right to express their view, but surely that does not mean an elected government has a mandate to do just anything between polls? What is the right balance between governments leading the people and following them?

One, two, three, four, we don't want your fascist war!

See also

26. The duck that won the lottery

Post hoc *fallacies*

The owner told us it was a lucky ducky and if stroked it would bring good luck on the lottery.

Martyn Frost, *Sun*[34]

When Martyn Frost's partner told him they had won nearly £1 million on the national lottery, he burst into tears. What was the secret of their success? The couple had stroked a lucky origami duck at the China Lounge restaurant in Whitefield, Greater Manchester. Sure enough, in the next draw, they won.

Frost sounded unconvinced that the duck actually caused his good fortune, but plenty of people are impressed when doing something superstitious is followed by a lucky break.

For example, Sulayman Ahmed[35] believed that buying a lucky phone number 'brought me so much luck it is unbelievable'. The only specific change of fortune mentioned in the newspaper report about him was that 'he has been relentlessly pursued by women desperate to go on dates with him'. None of these women was available for comment. The luckiest thing about the number seemed to be that Ahmed was going to be able to sell it on for even more and 'start buying property'.

Let us suppose that Ahmed did indeed have a lucky streak since buying the number. Does that prove it possesses magical properties? Does Martyn Frost's lottery win prove the paper bird was lucky? No, in both cases. The reason is simple enough, and those who think otherwise are committing a common error known as the '*post hoc* fallacy'.

Here's how it works. Think of a conditional statement of the form 'If X, then Y', such as 'If this is a lucky number, then owning it will bring me luck.' What happens if Ahmed actually enjoys good luck after buying the number is that he thinks this shows the truth of what is in the 'if' clause: 'This is a lucky number.' But it doesn't, because it is not true that he would have enjoyed the good luck only if the number were lucky. There could be other explanations. Luck is distributed randomly, most of us think, and at any given time there is a chance that you will enter into a lucky streak. So the subsequent run of good luck can never prove that what came before it was its cause.

The mistake is even easier to see in other examples. Imagine we are watching a football match and I say, 'If I scratch my leg there will be a goal in the next hour.' If I did scratch my leg and there was in fact a goal, very few people would think that the scratching was the cause of the goal.

It is remarkable, however, the extent to which people fall for the fallacy. They are quick to attribute causal powers to things that occurred before something else. Many superstitions start this way. Someone wears a hat for the first time and that day their football team wins. From that day on it is their lucky hat.

It is also amazing how blind people are to other much more obvious explanations. Ahmed, for example, could hardly have been indifferent to his religion when he bought the number, since he parted with £5,000 for the number on the basis of its religious significance. When he said that having the number helped him 'become more focused' on his religion, he seemed to be confusing cause and effect. And being convinced of its luck would certainly have given him a certain confidence that might translate into more success with women and in other areas of life.

The cases of a phone number and a duck may seem comic, but how many other times do we commit *post hoc* fallacies? If you take some kind of medicine, conventional or otherwise, does it really show the medicine worked if you subsequently get better? Does the fact that something bad happened when you said it wouldn't show that you mustn't 'tempt fate'? And does the fact that some people have committed great atrocities after becoming very religious show that religion inevitably leads to extremism?

See also

27. Does 6 million mean nothing to you?

Guilt by association

> That way lies eugenics, and we know from German history where that leads. We are already on that road: for what else is the termination of 6 million lives in the womb since the Abortion Act was introduced, and embryo selection on the basis of gender and genes?
>
> Cardinal Cormac Murphy-O'Connor[36]

Given that Cardinal Cormac Murphy-O'Connor is a Roman Catholic, it comes as no surprise to find that he is against abortion. But it is still something of a shock to hear him compare the termination of foetal life with Nazi eugenics programmes, which he has done on several occasions. In the quote above he even evokes a comparison with the Holocaust with his references to '6 million lives'.

The cardinal does not, however, offer very compelling arguments as to why we should see some kind of moral equivalence between eugenics and abortion (which are separate issues anyway), and Nazi atrocities. Perhaps he doesn't need to. Simply by making some kind of link between National Socialism and the practices he abhors, he succeeds in implying guilt by association: putting two things that have no necessary connection together in the hope that the bad name of one will taint the other.

The same trick can be applied to an astonishing array of beliefs and practices. The Nazis were very keen on ecology, forests, public rallies, compulsory gym classes and keep fit. If you yourself object to any of these, then slip in a mention of Nazi policy next time you want your criticisms to pack an added rhetorical punch. And if you're being bothered by a vegetarian while you're trying to enjoy your T-bone steak, just remind your critic that Hitler too eschewed meat.

The problem with guilt by association is that it fails to show what is actually wrong with the thing being criticized. The fact that some bad people like, support or do it does not add up to a criticism. Would love be bad if the devil had loved? Should books be banned because *Mein Kampf* too was a book? Should we not teach history and geography because that's what Pol Pot did? Of course not. Nothing is bad or wrong simply because the hand of evil has touched it. If it is wrong, you should show why it is wrong instead of resorting to innuendo to make it appear wrong by association.

Guilt by association can be implied much more subtly than this. For example, in 2002, it was widely reported that Clint Eastwood was suing a biographer for saying he was a wife-beater, a wartime coward and an atheist. That struck me as a very odd juxtaposition by the reporter. No one said that atheism was a comparable crime to wife-beating or cowardice. But at the very least there is something unsettling in the casual conjunction of the three. Would anyone be offended by the combination of wife-beater, coward and Jew in the same sentence? Would we really accept that no one was suggesting being a Jew was bad?

Guilt by association works because at some level we seem to accept the maxim that 'you shall be judged by the company you keep', directly or otherwise. And, indeed, there is some wisdom in this, even if it is too often exaggerated. If an idea or practice has proved to be popular among unsavoury sorts, it is at least worth stepping back and asking if there is something wrong with it. Suspicion by association, however, is not the same as guilt, and even suspicion needs to be tempered, to keep us from unwarranted prejudice.

When is suspicion by association appropriate? Is it rational or reasonable to ask why so many of the leading environmental campaigners in the UK – such as George Monbiot (son of promi-nent Tories, public school- and Oxford-educated), Jonathon Porritt (Eton), Zac Goldsmith (Eton), Prince Charles and Lord Melchett – are from the upper classes? Is this a clue as to the deep conservatism of the environmental movement or no more than a curious sociolog-ical accident? How far should we allow the mere association of green and blue to affect our thinking about their relationship? Jumping to conclusions would be rash, but so, surely, would be ignoring the link?

See also

28. Milk is for cows

Genetic fallacies

> Cow's milk is meant for baby cows. Which helps explain why this foodstuff is a leading cause of unwanted reactions to foods that can give rise to a variety of health issues such as nasal congestion, sinusitis, eczema and asthma.
>
> Dr John Briffa, *Observer Food Monthly*[37]

It's funny how the more common a foodstuff is, the more likely it is to be demonized by health-faddists. Wheat, cow's milk and tea are bad; but rye, goat's milk and herbal infusions are good. I smell a rat here, but it's not the rhetorical rodent that interests me most in Briffa's damning indictment of cow's milk. His mistake is the common one of jumping to unjustified conclusions about the present use or nature of something from facts about its origins.

By Briffa's logic, a chicken's thigh is meant to help it stand up and walk. Does that mean we should be wary about eating it because it wasn't meant for eating? What about honey, another favourite of health food shops? That was 'meant' for bees not humans. As for eggs, well, they were 'meant' to be baby animals, not omelettes. Even if we allow ourselves to talk loosely about what things in nature are 'meant' for, it should be obvious that this does not tell the whole story about what they can be used for.

The point is simple and obvious: the fact that something did not evolve as a human foodstuff does not mean we shouldn't eat it. In fact, if we ate only what was unambiguously meant for us to eat, then we'd starve to death as soon as we stopped breast-feeding.

More generally, nothing about something's present nature follows by logical necessity from facts about its origins. Consider how the etymology of words is often interesting but irrelevant to present usage. 'Generous', for example, has its origins in the Latin *generosus*, which means 'of noble birth'. But that doesn't mean that to say now that someone is generous implies something about their family background. Words change their meanings just as objects change their uses, so knowing an original use or meaning does not tell us what the current use or meaning is.

That is not to say that the history of a term is always entirely irrelevant. For example, water is the stuff we have always called 'water', which turns out to be H_2O. If we discovered something else that had all the appearance of being water, but it wasn't actually H_2O, it wouldn't be water. 'Water' is an example of what Saul Kripke called 'rigid designators': words whose meanings are fixed to the particular things or substances which they first named. Even so, our understanding of the nature of water changes over time and is not constrained by the pre-scientific ideas of those who first named it.

Appeals to origins have a strong rhetorical force, especially when they point to where ideas first germinated. If an idea or practice's origins can be traced back to the Nazis, the military, agribusiness or imperialism, it instantly becomes less attractive to many. Similarly, if something has its origins in 'nature', indigenous communities or social justice movements, it instantly gains credit among some. But although the history of an idea or practice may tell us something about its merits today, it need not do so. Nazis were early opponents of smoking, and on that they were right.

Origins shouldn't always be ignored, however. We are faced with many claims from different sources, and if we did not use our knowledge of the general reliability of these sources to at least determine which to take seriously, we would have no filter and we would soon be overwhelmed.

We are also justified in at least being suspicious of an idea on the basis of where it has come from. If a free market think tank reports that free markets are a good thing, we might at least question the objectivity of the research. Nevertheless, that research should stand or fall on its own merits.

It can be a worthwhile exercise to conduct an audit of our usual sources of information and check whether we apportion them the appropriate level of trust. Which sources do we trust too readily, and which do we dismiss too quickly? Imagine someone watching you from the outside: would they regard your own reflex responses to the credibility of information sources as being naïve or prejudiced?

See also

29. Murdered, yes; murderer, no

High redefinition

I am not a drink driver: it just happened to be a one-off.

Keith Floyd, celebrity chef[38]

Marion had never sung before in her life. Then one day at a pub karaoke, she bravely took to the stage, belted her lungs out and received an enthusiastic response from a crowd numbed from endless bad Whitney Houston impressions. 'I didn't know you were a karaoke singer,' said one of the punters. Marion replied, 'I'm not; it just happened to be a one-off.'

Geoff was one of the impressed drinkers. When he got home to the wife he hated, he found her drunk and singing 'My Heart Will Go On' in precisely the kind of way that makes you begrudgingly admire Celine Dion's vocal artistry. In a rage, he grabbed a kitchen knife and killed her. In court, he said, 'I'm not a murderer; it just happened to be a one-off.'

How many times do you need to do something to be classified as a doer of it? To be a singer, writer, painter or actor, for example, you need to have sung, written, painted or acted more than once. But if you murder, conquer, discover or visit just once, you are a murderer, conqueror, discoverer or visitor.

The rules vary from activity to activity and cannot be completely formalized. Consider what it means to be a winner. Sometimes, one win is enough. The England football team is a

World Cup winner by virtue of a sole victory back in 1966. In other contexts, however, we use the term 'winner' to describe someone who repeatedly wins. Often, it will be unclear which context applies.

Of course, so much of language is like this. The precise meanings of words can vary. Sometimes we exploit this in order to put a more favourable gloss on events. This is surely what happened in the case of Keith Floyd. Floyd had been driving while three and a half times over the legal alcohol limit, resulting in a head-on collision in a narrow country lane. Luckily, no one suffered more than minor injuries.

Does that make Floyd a drink-driver? That depends on whether the desription is more like 'murderer' or 'singer'. Context does mean that there is some latitude of usage here, but surely, in general, 'drink-driver' is more like 'murderer' (linguistically, not morally, of course). If someone is found guilty of drink-driving only once, they are described as a 'convicted drunk-driver'.

However, despite confessing he felt 'ashamed' and 'mortified', Floyd was reluctant to see himself as a drink-driver. Thus he shifted the meaning of the term so that it became narrower. So narrow, in fact, that it no longer applied to him.

This move is called 'high redefinition' and it's a common way of making credible denial possible. Perhaps the most common example is when people deny that they have deceived anyone. Usually, they do so by focusing on the requirement that deception requires intent. Then intent is defined so narrowly that even in a case where it could easily be foreseen that a misunderstanding would arise and the person did nothing to prevent it, deception is denied because that was not the clear, sole and specific aim of the person accused.

High redefinition is justified when there is a need to be revisionist with language and the revision is overt. For example, it could be argued that the term 'philosopher' has gradually become too widely used, so that all sorts of people can be described as one, irrespective of the quality of their original philosophizing. So should we attempt a corrective high redefinition, and in the process rob me of the right to the label? High redefinition may usually be a sneaky rhetorical move, but sometimes we need more of it.

The list of words and phrases which are potential candidates for justified high redefinition is pretty long. I would suggest 'health drink', 'star of stage and screen', 'best-selling author', 'crisis', 'quality ingredients', 'must-see television' and 'essential reading' for starters. Perhaps the worst is 'famous', as in signs like 'our famous Sunday roasts' which stand outside obscure pubs. What would be on your list?

See also

30. Dear, wise reader

Flattery

> See, I trust the American people. The American people are fantastic, great citizens. We've got to trust people with their own choices in life.
>
> George W. Bush[39]

> I trust the British people. I trust their common sense.
>
> William Hague, leader of the Conservative Party[40]

In 1937, one of the all-time best-selling self-improvement books was published. *How to Win Friends and Influence People* has sold more than 15 million copies and is now one of the most recognized titles in the world.

The book has little to do with the construction of sound arguments, but, nevertheless, perhaps more philosophers should read it. If they did so, they might realize why they have so little impact on the wider world. One of the fundamental techniques for handling people author Dale Carnegie suggested was 'Don't criticize, condemn or complain.' Philosophy without criticism is like hunting deer without a shotgun, so, if you want people to like you, avoid robust philosophical debate.

The second piece of core advice was 'Give people a feeling of importance.' In other words, flatter them. It sounds so crude, but it really does seem to work, just as long as the flattery does-n't appear too false. (If it sounds *just a little* phoney, you'll probably get the benefit of the doubt.) You see this in its most absurd form at rock concerts, where the band always seems to be especially happy to be performing in your town. One exam-ple which always makes me laugh is Eric Bloom's enthusiastic welcome to the crowd on a Blue Öyster Cult live album, when he says, 'We like coming up here from New York City because we know Poughkeepsie is serious about rock and roll!' That got a huge cheer. Mind you, perhaps he was being honest: when the former stadium-fillers performed in the even more modest venue of my home town of Folkestone, he said, 'We've never played here before. I don't know why,' in a tone which sug-gested he knew perfectly well.

Such flattery is not only confined to low culture, however. Authors at book festivals often say similar things to their audi-ences, and I can't believe they're all being entirely honest. (Apart from me, of course.) Politicians also play the flattery card. The most common trick, especially by conservatives, is to say that our lot trust you and the others don't. The crude message is, would you prefer a government that thinks you're too dumb to make important life choices for yourself or do you want one which appreciates your wisdom and intelligence? I know which I would prefer.

But more often than not, this rhetoric is empty. The trust conservative governments have in the people is extremely selec-tive. Bush vetoed legislation permitting stem cell research, which did not show a great deal of trust in scientific and med-ical professionals to make ethical choices. He withdrew America from the UN Population Fund, not trusting people to make their own choices on reproductive issues. He also signed the No

Child Left Behind Act, which was more, not less, prescriptive on what and how schools should teach. Whatever the merits of these decisions, they do not square with the simple story he likes to tell of how he trusts people while the Democrats don't.

British Conservatives are no different. They prefer a tax system which encourages marriage, not trusting people to make up their own minds for personal reasons whether they would rather wed or not. They also introduced a national curriculum for schools, giving more power to the Westminster education departments than local schools. Again, the simple 'we trust you more' message doesn't wash.

Although flattery is a cheap trick which often works, there are some who think that being a no-nonsense, rational kind of person means you should avoid any attempts at politeness at all. Just say what you mean and mean what you say: all else is mere fluff.

But some of Carnegie's techniques serve the pursuit of truth as well as they do the pursuit of favour. 'If you're wrong, admit it quickly and emphatically,' he advised. Perhaps most importantly, 'Try honestly to see things from the other person's point of view.' That's not just being nice, it's necessary if you actually want to get somewhere in a conversation. While it is true that we have to be wary of people being nice to us for nefarious ends, that doesn't mean not being nice is the hallmark of intellectual rigour.

Here's a project that someone should carry out for real. (If someone already has, please let me know.) At an election, rate each candidate's speeches according to the number of times they flatter their electorate. Not only would the results be interesting in their own right, it would be fascinating to see how and if they correlated with success. We can all try a scaled-down version of this: just listen out for flattery in political speeches and question-time panels on radio and television. The depressing thing is, it usually gets applause.

See also

31. What would Brian Boitano say?

Arguments from authority

> As a result of the work of Christian philosophers such as
> Alvin Plantinga, it is widely recognized that the internal
> problem of evil is a failure as an argument for atheism.
>
> William Lane Craig, theologian[41]

When we were children, we spoke as children, we understood as children, we thought as children; and when we became adults, we pretended to put away childish things. In the playgrounds of schools all over the world, we see in their purest, most undiluted forms, patterns of thought and behaviour that persist right through a lifetime. Observe, for instance, this typical exchange:

> 'My dad says Toyotas are much better than Volvos.'
> 'Well, your dad is stupid.'

It is a rare grown-up who still refers to his father as an authority in disputes, but rarer still is one who does not defer to authorities at all. Just as young kids often take their parents' opinions as the final arbiters in disagreements, adults sometimes appeal to the opinions of those they admire, as though that somehow settles it. But it does not, of course.

No one would mistake the serious theologian William Lane

Craig for a bratty youth, but even he is not above settling a dispute with a swift citation of expert opinion. In *The Cambridge Companion to Philosophy*, Craig dismisses what he calls the internal problem of evil simply by informing us that 'it is widely recognized' that it fails to disprove the existence of God. He comes pretty close to saying it's true because Alvin Plantinga says so.

Even if Craig is right, it is no argument at all simply to invoke the authority of probably the best Christian philosopher working today. Nor is it a reasonable defence in this instance for him to say that his job was merely to report the consensus: his appeal to authority stood out in a book which generally took time to explain arguments, albeit sometimes in telegraphic form.

Surely, however, there is a difference between saying 'because Plantinga and other leading lights say so' and 'because my dad says so'? Isn't it sometimes necessary to bow down before people who know more about a subject than you do?

Yes, with qualification. We should resort to relying on authorities only when we are unable to follow an argument, so in that sense an 'argument from authority' is a misnomer: it is actually using an authority instead of an argument.

What then counts as being genuinely unable to follow an argument? Sometimes it is a basic lack of ability. If you find maths hard, then even if a mathematician could explain to you why Fermat's last theorem has been solved, you wouldn't be able to understand her. So if you need to decide whether it has been solved or not, you can do no more than see what expert witnesses say.

On other occasions our inability to understand is due to a lack of time, either because we don't have enough minutes free to read or hear the full explanation, or because we don't have the years required to study the subject long enough to truly understand it. Again, in these circumstances, the testimony of experts is the best we can go on.

In both cases, however, relying on experts is a necessary evil. In general, passing the buck, intellectually speaking, is something to be avoided.

It is not always clear whether we understand enough to assess the evidence for ourselves or whether we really should trust others. Global warming is a good example: all the national academies of science of the major industrialized countries agree that global warming is real and mainly caused by human activity. Yet still, many people who are not experts believe they understand enough about the issue to see that there are serious doubts about the truth of this conclusion. When there is such a conflict between the mass of expert opinion and what our own intellects tell us, how should we choose? Is it arrogant to deny the expert opinion of so many, or is it an abdication of responsibility to allow one's one reason to be over-ruled?

See also

50. Vacuous pseudo-wisdom
66. False authorities
83. Appeals to common sense
88. Fallacy of ancient wisdom

32. Reading between the lines

'It sends the wrong message'

Making the morning-after pill available to all girls over six-teen in this way sends the wrong message about the need for responsible sexual activity. It can only increase the risk of worsening the current epidemic of sexually transmitted disease.

Dr Liam Fox, shadow health secretary[42]

The UK has one of the highest rates of unwanted teen pregnancies and teenage parents in Europe. Of course, if the little blighters would stop having sex, this would soon cease to be the case. However, promoting abstinence is both morally problematic (not least because most adults do not disapprove of sex outside marriage for themselves) and ineffective. An Oxford University study showed that abstinence programmes in the US, such as the Silver Ring Thing, had no effect on rates of STD infection or unprotected sex.[43] Another study, published in the *Journal of Adolescent Health*, suggested that boys who took the abstinence pledge were four times more likely to engage in anal sex than those who did not pledge.[44]

Two alternatives are to spread the message that if you do have sex, it should be 'safe' (without giving the false impression that it will therefore be risk-free); and to provide easy access to morning-after contraception for those who fail to use condoms or whose condoms have failed. This latter measure was proposed by the UK government, which wanted 'emergency contraception' to be made available to girls over sixteen without prescription or parental permission. It was widely welcomed by family-planning professionals and family doctors.

'Pro-family' and anti-abortion groups didn't like this, of course. If you really do believe that the morning-after pill causes abortion, and abortion is murder, you obviously wouldn't want society to condone either practice. But there was one argument, invoked by the Conservative health spokesperson Liam Fox, which didn't ring true. He claimed that this measure would 'send the wrong message'.

This argument is often used when liberalizing laws are proposed. You heard it a lot when cannabis was reclassified from class B to the less serious class C status. It was claimed this would send the message that cannabis was safe, when in fact it wasn't.

Obviously this was not the official message. All that reclassifying cannabis overtly did was inform the public that the authorities believed cannabis was not as dangerous as amphetamines, but in the same broad category of risk as ketamine and GHB. People could read more between the lines if they wished, but nothing was written there.

Similarly, no message need be sent by making access to the morning-after pill easier, other than the fact that collectively society thinks this is a morally acceptable way to help deal with unwanted pregancies. Why see the message as being 'Risky sex is fine, kids' when it could just as easily be 'We've decide to provide more help for the idiots who don't play it safe the first time'? If you think that people are likely to draw the wrong conclusion from such a law, you can always send an overt message to counter that. This is arguably what should have happened with cannabis reclassification. Two years after the change, Home Secretary Charles Clarke decided there needed to be a publicity campaign to warn people of the dangers, but refused to change back the classification of the drug. This seemed to be an acknowledgement that, although the change was right, people read the wrong message into it. The two things, however, need not necessarily have gone together.

Sometimes laws are all about sending messages. A notorious example is Section 28, a piece of UK legislation enacted in 1986 by the Conservatives and repealed in 2003 (2000 in Scotland). The law prohibited the promotion of homosexuality by local authorities. No successful prosecution was ever brought under its provision, but arguably that was not the point: it was always mainly about symbolism, 'sending a message' that councils should not be too supportive of gay rights. Repealing the amendment thus also became a symbolic rejection of this alleged homophobia.

So although it is often claimed that measures send a message which they needn't do, sometimes the whole point of a political act is symbolic. When someone objects that something sends the wrong message, we therefore need to ask first whether a message is being sent at all, and only then whether it should be changed.

Many acts do send a message, whether we like it or not. But people disagree as to what those messages are. Do parents who let their teenage children smoke at home send a message that they can't stop what their children will do and respect them even if they disagree with it; or that they don't feel strongly enough about their self-destructive behaviour? Does continuing to offer help to a relative who keeps screwing up send a positive message of unconditional support, or does it signal that the relation need never take full responsibility for their actions?

See also

33. Moderates need not apply

Distorting to balance

> For some time now Oxfam and Christian Aid have given
> donors the chance to give a present by sponsoring a farm
> animal in the developing world [. . .] Not everyone thinks
> that's a very good idea: Andrew Tyler is director of Animal
> Aid, and he's one of those; Jane Moyo is a spokesperson for
> ActionAid.
>
> James Naughtie, *Today* programme[45]

I am sometimes contacted by a researcher for a radio or television programme as a potential contributor to some kind of
topical debate. Often nothing comes of the initial discussion.
But on more than one occasion the reason for my unsuitability
has left me concerned. As one researcher explicitly said and
others have implied, I am not extreme enough in my views.

This woke me up to the fact that all too often 'balance' in
a debate is interpreted to mean, first, to give both sides of the
argument equal opportunity to present their views; and second,
to represent both sides at their most trenchant. But does this
really present a balanced picture?

In one sense, of course it does: there is balance because
there are two equal and opposite opinions. But the point of
striving for balance is surely to represent the debate fairly. And
I'm not sure this approach achieves that goal.

For one thing, sometimes issues just aren't as contested as this approach suggests. Scientific opinion is rarely divided 50–50, but the usual kind of balanced debate can give the false impression that it is.

On other occasions, the truth is distorted by getting two people with polarized, fixed views to thrash issues out. Sometimes this is nonetheless worth doing, to provoke challenging debate, but in the example from the *Today* programme, I can't help but think their choice of guests would not be the most illuminating. Animal Aid is not keen on animals being used for human ends at all, and ActionAid offers the opportunity to sponsor farm animals. No prizes, then, for guessing the positions taken by their representatives on whether it is moral to sponsor farm animals in the developing world.

The problem is that most issues are really clear-cut only for those who, like the two contributors, stand at the extreme poles of the disagreement. Many others would get more from a debate which dealt with the complexities of an issue rather than simply ping-ponging between two extreme views.

Presenting a debate in terms of the two strongest cases that can be made on either side is particularly dangerous in issues of great sensitivity, such as the decision by the Birmingham Repertory Theatre to cancel performances of the play *Behzti* because of violent protests by Sikhs who found scenes of a rape in a temple to be offensive. Talking about this on *Today* were Evan Harris of the National Secular Society and Dr Jasdev Rai, director of the Sikh Human Rights Group.[46] Again, neither the positions taken nor the arguments offered in support of them were at all surprising. Worse still, presenting the argument as a clash of fundamentals exacerbated the sense that there was a huge gulf between the Sikh community and the majority. In reality, however, most people in both camps probably agreed about a great deal. Glossing over this could have increased tensions between and within communities.

The *Today* programme is not a prime offender in this regard, and it could be argued that the examples I have chosen are just part of a mix in which many other more independent voices are heard. But in the media in general, the formula of soliciting two equal and opposite views is the one that is almost invariably followed. The cumulative effect of all these discussions is to present a picture of a society which is dominated by adversarial conflicts and huge gulfs. Consensus and the moderate middle ground, occupied by the majority, are left unrepresented, and so the striving for balance actually fails to reflect the real balance of the opinions that are out there.

It would not be much of an improvement, of course, if we went too far the other way and every discussion were conducted only between moderates. Getting the right balance of debaters required to achieve balance is not easy.

When you look at how debates are presented in the media you use, do you think they are even close to providing the right balance? Try listening to or watching your favourite broadcast news programme and pay more attention than usual to who they have on to provide comment. How many times does their attempt at balance accurately represent opinion, and how often does it actually distort the reality?

See also

34. If only I'd known

Post facto *rationalizations*

Had I known then what I know now, I would not have been able to vote for that motion.

Michael Howard, leader of the Conservative Party[47]

Had I known this at the time, I never would have voted for this war.

Senator John Edwards[48]

Had I known then what I know now, I would not have voted that way.

Harriet Harman, deputy leader of the Labour Party [49]

Many politicians and commentators supported the decision to invade Iraq in 2003. And a lot of them came to regret that choice. The invasion went well enough, but the aftermath has been a long, bloody struggle. For many, in retrospect, it seems that they backed the wrong horse.

It's hard to admit one was wrong over a big issue. Harder still to maintain that one was right when the cost in human lives has been so high. So it is understandable that many have tried to backtrack. And fortunately for them, they have been offered a way out: it transpires that the intelligence reports which suggested Saddam had weapons of mass destruction were totally wrong. This means that the likes of John Edwards, Harriet Harman and Michael Howard are now able to say that they would never have backed the invasion of Iraq if they had been given accurate information. They were misled, and so, although it is true they supported a misguided military adventure, you can't blame them for that.

One problem with this kind of counterfactual history is that there is simply no way of knowing whether the hypothetical being claimed is accurate. It's not just that we cannot know whether people are telling the truth; if they were honest, most people who say they would have done otherwise can't really know if this is the case. We can be judged only on what we actually do, not on what we say we would have done.

These unproven hypotheticals are often bogus. Rather than being genuine accounts of what we would have done, they are *post facto* rationalizations for mistakes. A *post facto* rationalization is a way of making sense of what has happened after the event which misdescribes what really happened. They are very common in sports reports, where the role of chance is often played down and other, less random, factors are given an elevated role in the explanation of results. For instance, in the 1999 UEFA Champions League final between Manchester United and Bayern Munich the British team trailed 1–0 for almost the entire game. But remarkably, they scored two goals in three minutes of injury time and won the cup. Commentator Clive Tyldesley responded to the first of these goals with the exclamation 'Name on the trophy!' And, indeed, post-match reports talked about United's win as though it were an inevitability, when in fact it hinged on a combination of determination and sheer luck.

In the more serious case of voting for war in Iraq, it is impossible to say which, if any, out of Edwards, Harman and Howard were engaged in *post facto* rationalization. But surely at least some others who claim they would have acted differently are kidding themselves. In the build-up to the war, Saddam's alleged possession of WMD was just one factor cited by those in favour of an invasion. The official reason was a failure to comply with the terms of UN resolutions: Saddam had not been co-operating with weapons inspectors, a fact few would dispute. But in retrospect, many people now maintain that the critical factor was the WMD claim. Is it really too cynical to suggest that the reason they place emphasis on this is not because it was actually the determining factor in their choice, but because it is the one thing they can now distance themselves from?

We're all prone to *post facto* rationalizations, since they help us to live with uncomfortable truths about the past. But when we look back at our decisions, can we truthfully say that we always 'only had the interests of other people at heart'? When we say we 'did what seemed best at the time', did we try hard enough to find out what really was best? Might we be more honest if we stood up and said that sometimes we did the wrong thing for the wrong reasons and we could and should have done better?

See also

35. Coffee enema conquers cancer

Begging the question

> [Dudley Poplak] gave [Prince] Charles a copy of the book *A Time to Heal: My Triumph over Cancer* – Beata Bishop's story of how she beat malignant melanoma twenty-three years ago by following the strict dietary regime.
>
> Jo Revill, *Observer*[50]

Beata Bishop's 'strict dietary regime' was the Gerson Therapy, which eschews drugs in favour of coffee enemas and fruit juices. It has the support of well-known medical experts such as Prince Charles, interior designer Dudley Poplak and educationalist Lord Baldwin of Bewdley. Their opinions, of course, carry more weight than those of the American Cancer Society, which warns that the treatment could be dangerous.

To say that the Gerson Therapy is controversial is therefore something of an understatement. Unfortunately for the public, however, Prince Charles was able to use his authority to support the treatment, a move which understandably 'infuriated the medical establishment'.

Good reporting of health issues is important, because people often make important choices on the basis of what they read in what they believe to be respectable newspapers. Jo Revill is generally quite careful, but even she tripped up when she reported that Bishop 'beat' cancer 'by following the strict dietary regime'. This description begs the question: it assumes precisely what is being contested. What Revill should have said is that Bishop got better while following the diet. The facts indicate a temporal coincidence, not a causal link.

Although my correction may seem pedantic, it is crucial. For what Revill's form of words implies is that on at least one occasion the therapy did work. That means the controversy is transformed into a debate about how often it works and how reliable it is, when it really should be concerned with whether it works at all.

Begging the question – assuming what needs to be argued for – is often a result of a careless use of language. It can occur when we use 'success' words where more neutral vocabulary is needed. For example, we say *learned* French when really we only *studied* it and never developed any real competence. Republicans say that Ronald Reagan *won* the Cold War, when perhaps the Cold War simply ended while he was president. A military retaliation may achieve little, but it is still said to have *avenged* an attack. When we learn, win or avenge, we achieve something by our actions. No such success is implied by the fact that we study, retaliate or simply have power. The unjustified use of success words is not the same mistake as begging the question, but it is often the means by which question-begging occurs, as it was when it was erroneously granted that Bishop 'beat' cancer with Gerson Therapy.

What is the difference between begging the question and a benign granting that the case has been won? Must I say that drinking only appeared to destroy an alcoholic's liver, because I can't rule out other causes completely? Until recently, many would not have thought that saying Prozac alleviated someone's depression begged the question. But research published in 2008 questioning the usefulness of modern antidepressants in all but the most severe cases suggests that is exactly what such a statement does.[51] Unless we are prepared tiresomely to attach endless provisos to what we say, aren't we inevitably going to have to beg some questions some of the time?

See also

36. It's OK – I understand

Explanation is not justification

As bizarre as some of these facts may seem, they all make sense when rape is viewed as a natural, biological phenomenon that is a product of the human evolutionary heritage.

Evolutionary biologist Randy Thornhill and evolutionary anthropologist Craig Palmer[52]

One of the most controversial academic books of recent years is *A Natural History of Rape: Biological Bases of Sexual Coercion* by Randy Thornhill and Craig Palmer. Thornhill and Palmer argued that to explain rape and why it is so common, it is more helpful to view it as an evolved reproductive strategy for males than it is to see it as purely misogynistic violence with no goal other than humiliation, domination or perverse pleasure.

Thornhill and Palmer believe this theory better explains numerous otherwise puzzling empirical facts about rape (the 'bizarre' facts mentioned above), such as that 'Most rape victims are women of childbearing age', 'In many cultures rape is treated as a crime against the victim's husband' and 'Rape takes place not only among human beings but also in a variety of other animal species.'

Many have accused Thornhill and Palmer of justifying rape;

that by claiming it is 'natural' they somehow make it morally acceptable. In response, the authors have pointed out that *explaining* something is not the same as *justifying* it.

For instance, getting a conviction for a murder requires establishing a motive, the means and an opportunity for the killing. Together these facts explain the homicide, but of course they don't justify it. Quite the opposite: such an explanation is required to punish someone for the crime.

There are certainly times when people do feel that explanations militate against condemnation. For example, we are often told that most child abusers were abused themselves, and this, in some sense, inevitably tends to lead to the conclusion that we should have sympathy for the abuser as well as his (usually it is a he) victim.

But even here there is a vital distinction: the explanation may make us treat the perpetrator more sympathetically, but it in no way makes their crime any less heinous. Thornhill and Palmer's argument might make us less optimistic about the possibility of eradicating rape completely from society, but it does not in any way make the crime less serious. Furthermore, the fact that rape norms vary enormously across cultures and that the vast majority of men do not rape suggest that we have no reason to be softer on rapists either.

If evolutionary psychology does reinforce inequality, then that is more due to psychology than logic. As a matter of fact, people do seem to make an easy leap between explanation and justification. Perhaps it is because they think many explanations of behaviour show that things must be the way they are, and we are thus foolish to change them. If men are from Mars and women are from Venus, isn't it crazy to try to change their Venusian and Martian ways?

If an explanation of human behaviour really pointed to immutable facts of human nature, this argument would be right. But this is not how most explanations of behaviour work. In fact, we know that gender roles in particular are quite variable. Scandinavian countries, for example, have been very successful at getting men and women to share domestic and child-rearing work, which have traditionally been seen as more feminine. At most, some explanations might suggest the limits on this malleability. What they can't do is justify acts that we know we are not compelled to carry out.

How far, if at all, should knowledge of what is 'natural' affect our social policies? For instance, it has been hypothesized that there is wider variability among male than female brains, which would mean men were likely to provide more of society's geniuses but also more of its dunces. If this were true, shouldn't we revise our expectations of 50–50 representation of men and women in the highest positions in society? Or should we still push for this for other reasons?

See also

51. Legality and morality
59. 'I was just doing my job'
65. Cause is not responsibility
71. How else do you explain it?

37. The only way is down

The regressive fallacy

The unemployment rate – still too high – is the lowest in nearly seven years, and our people have created nearly 13 million new jobs.

Ronald Reagan[53]

Reaganomics has never been short of its detractors, but as Reagan said in his 1987 State of the Union Address, unemployment under his presidency fell to a seven-year low. Surely he was doing something right?

Maybe he was. But the data alone doesn't prove that he was. In 1982, a year after Reagan took office, US unemployment was at a post-war high of 9.7 per cent. It could have gone higher, but the chances were that sooner or later, probably sooner, it would start to fall. The reason for this is what statisticians call 'regression to the mean': when you measure something and find it is at an extreme, it is always probable that the next time you measure it, it will probably be less extreme. So when unemployment did indeed start to fall again, was that because of Reagan's policies or in spite of them? After all, at 6.2 per cent, the unemployment rate in 1987 under Regan was still high by historical standards. In the year after he left office, unemployment started to rise again, before any effects of the new regime could have kicked in.

So the claim that 'our people have created nearly 13 million new jobs' seems dubious to say the least. It is possible that this is indeed what happened, but it is also possible that this is an example of the regressive fallacy: believing that actions you perform at the peak of a cycle are responsible for that peak passing. A typical example is when you have a cold and start taking medicine. Colds usually pass of their own accord, and there is no cure for them. But because people usually start to take medicines when they feel near their worst, and then they start getting better, they tend to think that the medicine had something to do with it. The same is true of all but the worst diseases, which is why many people swear by remedies that don't actually work.

The same fallacy makes assessing the effectiveness of treatments for depression very difficult. People tend to go to doctors or therapists only when they hit rock bottom. Given that it is not possible to feel any worse, and most people avoid the temptation of suicide, most are likely to feel better several months later. So how can we tell if the therapy or drugs really helped? There are ways, but you have to be very careful.

Regression to the mean is not some weird law of nature which says everything will even out in the long run. Sometimes, the peaks in the cycle just keep getting higher, as was the case with unemployment under Margaret Thatcher's Conservative government in the early 1980s. People thought it was terrible when it reached a post-war high of nearly 5 per cent under the previous Labour government, but it kept rising for several years, to over 10 per cent in 1986.

In the case of Reagan, it is hard to know whether unemployment would have kept on rising even higher had he not implemented his economic policies. And it would be plain foolish to assume that fears of rising global temperatures can be discounted because 'what goes up must come down'. Regression to the mean is strictly a matter of what is probable: nothing can be predicted or explained with certainty on the basis of it.

Being aware of the regressive fallacy is thus essentially a matter of being cautious about jumping to conclusions over what caused something to fall or rise from a peak state. We need to take it on a case by case basis to work out whether someone's actions were a true cause.

Is anyone to blame for the relative poor quality of *The Simpsons* from series nine, or is it simply the case that no one could maintain the level of excellence exhibited in the golden era of series four to eight? How much are the actions of the US military responsible for rises and falls in levels of violence in Iraq? And in both cases, isn't it likely that neither a natural regression to the mean nor deliberate action entirely explains what happened but that both played a role? In which case, how significant was either?

See also

16. The gambler's fallacy
26. *Post hoc* fallacies
43. Correlation is not causation
52. Failing to disaggregate

38. You should do the impossible

Ought without can

In 1998, Americans recoiled in horror after the shooting dead of four students and a teacher at a school in Jonesboro, Arkansas. Politicians, church leaders and ordinary members of the community said that it should never be allowed to happen again.

BBC News Online[54]

The principle that 'ought' implies 'can' is usually attributed to Immanuel Kant, although he never actually said anything quite so pithy. The principle itself is pretty self-evident: it makes no sense to say we ought to do something unless we can actually do it. It is absurd to say 'You ought to be eight foot tall' or 'You ought to eradicate world poverty by lunch time' since neither of these is a genuine possibility. How can you have a duty to do what is impossible?

The logic of the principle is clear enough, and frequently ignored. People call on politicians to do things that are not within their power or athletes to perform above their capabilities. For instance, in Britain, many people felt that the world's greatest woman distance runner, Paula Radcliffe, ought to have performed better at the Athens Olympics, where she retired from the two races in which she competed. What they don't seem to have taken seriously is the probability that Radcliffe was performing as well as she could.

The example of Paula Radcliffe is instructive, because although the 'ought' implies 'can' principle is crystal clear in theory, in the real world 'impossible' carries more than one sense, some looser than others. Radcliffe could never have run the marathon in one hour, not because it is *logically* impossible but because it is *physically* impossible. In ordinary discourse, it is perfectly legitimate to say something is not *practically* possible even though there is nothing either physically or logically preventing us doing it. Radcliffe could almost certainly have finished the race if she had put her all into it. Can we not therefore say that it is wrong to think she ought to have finished the race because it was unreasonable or unrealistic to expect her to have done so, though not strictly impossible?

That may seem to extend the reach of 'ought' implies 'can' too much. We have moved from can't (logically) through can't (physically) to can't (realistically) where the notion of what is 'realistic' is somewhat vague. It would certainly be accurate to describe this version of the principle as an adjunct or extension of the core one and not simply a corollary of it. But I think we need something like it in order to make the principle really effective in critical thinking about the real world.

Consider, for example, the plea that events such as the Jonesboro school killings should never be allowed to happen again. It is not at all obvious that any society could realistically ensure this. Banning all firearms in a country like the USA is not a politically viable option, and even if you did so, making sure there weren't any in illegal circulation is something no government has achieved. Then there is the issue of school security, which can never be as strict as, say, that in airports.

We can see the 'ought' implies 'can' principle therefore as having two versions. One concerns the link between duty and what is logically or physically possible and should be uncontroversial. But arguably the more interesting and useful version, though also the more controversial and imprecise one, is that we cannot say people ought to do what realistically speaking they cannot.

The philosopher Simon Critchley has argued that, in fact, ought implies cannot.[55] What he means is that a properly demanding morality always asks more of us than we can possible give. The insight of Christian theology is that we are doomed always to fall short of what we really ought to do. It's an intriguing suggestion. But even if it is true, isn't it nonetheless the case that in many practical cases, such as the political, we really shouldn't demand what cannot be done? Or are we better off asking for the impossible of those who will inevitably fall short?

See also

39. Lumping it all together

False singulars

> Therapy today, like the wider culture of which it is a part, teaches people to know their place. All that it offers in return are the dubious blessings of affirmation and recognition.
>
> Frank Furedi, *Therapy Culture*[56]

The human habit of categorizing often gets a bad press. We are told that we should avoid stereotypes and not pigeonhole people. The desire to place things into neat categories is seen as a pathological resistance to the messy reality of the world.

But a language which has a name for every individual thing but no words to group them is not one which can be used to make proper sense of the world. Science and philosophy are all about categorizing things better, and that often means making new and finer distinctions. It was progress when stuff was divided into the four elements, and progress again when chemistry broke down matter into the 117 elements that make up the periodic table.

The ideal we strive for is as many categories as are required to divide the world up accurately, but as few as we can get away with to do this efficiently. When we err, however, we tend to do so on the side of too few, not too many. In particular, we are drawn towards the binary. So, for example, we talk of complementary and conventional medicine, and in doing so lump together the absurdity of Reiki with the clinically tested St John's wort. Xenophobes talk about natives and immigrants, even though in countries like the US and UK, hardly anyone can claim a pure indigenous line. Even when we extend our categories to three, they are often woefully inadequate, such as the UK government's ridiculous attempt to label foods with a red, orange or green light to sum up their nutritional value.

The sociologist Frank Furedi has done some dubious lumping together in his attacks on what he calls the 'therapy culture'. Furedi has plenty of genuinely interesting and worthwhile things to say about how the privileging of emotion undermines self-reliance and pathologizes ordinary unhappiness. But he does his argument a disservice when he tars all forms of therapy with the same brush. In the final sentences of his book *Therapy Culture*, Furedi makes no attempt to distinguish between different forms of therapy, and simply talks about therapy in what we might call the false singular. Therapy, we are told, keeps people in their place and offers only recognition and affirmation.

Some of this is probably true of some therapies. Psychoanalysis, for example, has been accused of keeping clients in a dependence relationship by its insistence on very long, open-ended treatment, and by its implication that the therapist knows the patient better than she knows herself. But many forms of therapy are explicitly designed to get people out of it as soon as possible. Similarly, although some counselling does little more than validate the emotions of the client, the best kind challenges people and offers the possibility of changing the way they view themselves and their problems.

Furedi must know this, but in presenting his thesis in easily digestible, broad brushstrokes, he glosses over these distinctions. Such simplifications are sometimes benign or unavoidable: for example, earlier I talked about psychoanalysis in the false singular, as my broad point applied to Freudian, Jungian, Kleinian and Lacanian analysis, and numerous other variants. But in Furedi's case I think it was unnecessary and inaccurate to talk of therapy as though it were monolithic.

As is often the case, judgement is required to determine when generalization is desirable or disastrous. Without fairly broad categories, we can talk only of particulars; when they are too broad, we can talk only in falsehoods.

When is it acceptable to use a singular term for something we know in reality contains much variation? When, if at all, is it fair to make broad judgements about Christianity, Islam, terrorism, charities, politicians, reality TV, Impressionist painters, merchant bankers, British values or New Yorkers? When you make such judgements, are you being fair or too simplistic?

See also

40. Love George, hate terrorists

False dichotomies

> Every nation in every region now has a decision to make.
> Either you are with us, or you are with the terrorists.
>
> George W. Bush[57]

At first sight, George W. Bush's bold statement, made shortly after the attack on the World Trade Center in 2001, is a glaring example of a false dichotomy: presenting two options as though these exhausted all the possibilities, when in fact there are other choices available. There was at least one obvious alternative to Bush's choice, which was to oppose terrorism but also to oppose America's preferred methods of dealing with it. A person or country that adopted that line was not with President Bush, but neither were they with the terrorists.

Simple, isn't it? Well, not really. First, on a charitable interpretation of Bush's speech, he wasn't trying to suggest that the choice was so stark. He continued by saying, 'From this day forward, any nation that continues to harbour or support terrorism will be regarded by the United States as a hostile regime.' This suggests that not being 'with us' requires acquiescence with terrorists rather than a mere failure to support US policy. Indeed, when Bush repeated the dichotomy a few weeks later, in the context of a crackdown on terrorist finances, the main message again seemed to be that turning a blind eye to terrorism counted as being against America in its fight against it.

However, if this is true, why did Bush not only choose these particular words but also chose to repeat the same formulation again? The answer could be that as a description of the facts the dichotomy is false, but as a description of America's intentions it sent out a clear message. Bush was not describing the logic of agreement, but issuing an ultimatum. America made the untruth of the false dichotomy true by deciding that it would treat all those who were not with her as being against her, whether they saw themselves in that way or not. No wonder many Europeans accused Bush's administration of adopting a bullying attitude.

The false dichotomy is a great simplifier. It cuts out all the complexity of an issue and presents just two choices, take 'em or leave 'em. As a rhetorical trick, it is very common and not limited to dichotomies. Christian evangelical literature, for instance, often employs what we might call a false trichotomy. Christ, they say, claimed to be the son of God. He must have been telling the truth, lying or mad. There is no evidence that he was a liar or mad, so therefore he must have been telling the truth.

Of course, the problem is that the options presented don't exhaust the possibilities. Jesus may well not have claimed any such thing – the Gospels may be unreliable. He may also have meant something more metaphorical. After all, in Genesis it is said that 'When men began to increase in number on the earth and daughters were born to them, the sons of God saw that the daughters of men were beautiful, and they married any of them they chose' (6:1-2). So, clearly, for Bible believers, being the son of God isn't the unique achievement of Jesus. For these reasons and more, there are more than the three options presented.

However, we could easily get over-zealous about wiping out these logical aberrations. If we were to be too strict in our policing of false dichotomies, we would be robbed of some great quotes. 'Life is either a great adventure or nothing,' said Helen Keller. Well, no, but I see her point and it wouldn't have quite the same ring suitably qualified. Ditto Anthony Robbins's maxim, 'In life you need either inspiration or desperation.' Better still, Max Lerner's warning, 'Either men will learn to live like brothers, or they will die like beasts,' is no less forceful for being literally false.

All this reminds me of another false dichotomy: either one must speak with logical exactitude at all times or truth and reason will be swept aside by rhetoric and vagueness.

Do you think the following are false dichotomies or tough choices that have to be made: more security or more liberty? Slower economic growth or more environmental destruction? Fidelity or excitement? Vegetarianism or cruelty to animals?

See also

41. Knowledge in retrospect

Prediction is not foresight

Diana 'foresaw death crash'

Evening Standard front-page headline[58]

Hindsight may be a wonderful thing, but foresight is even better. What a pity, then, that people have foresight only in hindsight.

When people claim to foresee something, they generally mean one of two things. One is that they have real knowledge of the future: they can see it before it happens. No one actually has this kind of foresight, although many claim they do. The reason why I am so confident of this is that it would be easy to establish genuine foresight beyond reasonable doubt. All our prophet would have to do is make predictions consistently more accurate than chance or those of experts. But no one has done this, or even come close. Even famous seers such as Nostradamus made absurdly vague prophecies.

The other main use of the idea of foresight is an analogous one, where we don't really know what is going to happen, but we are so confident we speak in the language of prophets. This is no more than a colourful, hyperbolic way of saying you predict something will happen.

However, when we do predict something and we turn out to be right, suddenly we are much more likely to say we actually foresaw it. 'I told you!' we say, using a verb which suggests what we said was a fact before it even happened.

This is the kind of rewriting of history that was used to describe Princess Diana's uncanny remarks about a car crash. Underneath the headline 'Diana "foresaw death crash"', the *London Evening Standard* reported that in a handwritten note Diana had said, 'They're planning "an accident" in my car, brake failure and serious head injury in order to make the path clear for Charles to marry.'

You might think that using the verb 'foresaw' is quite harmless, but the Diana case is an excellent example of why we should not be so sanguine about such things. The idea that she in some way knew what was going to happen has been used to support conspiracy theories. But it is not only the false sense of certainty that is misleading about the use of 'foresaw', the verb also overestimates the extent to which her worries actually matched the events that later occurred. The only detail she gave was brake failure, which was not the cause of the accident that killed her. Worse than this, when the full text of the letter was later made public, it transpired she had written, 'My husband is planning "an accident" in my car, brake failure or some serious head injury in order to make the path clear for him to marry Tiggy. Camilla is nothing more than a decoy so we are being used by the man in every sense of the word.' But Charles didn't marry Tiggy (Legge-Bourke, Harry's nanny), he married Camilla. So much for Diana's foresight.

Even if Diana had been exactly correct, it would still have been inaccurate to describe her prediction as foresight. A prediction or an inkling is not knowledge, and it is not turned into knowledge by the fact of it coming true. If I were to predict next week's football scores, the chances are I would get some right, but it would not be accurate to say after the event that my predictions could be divided between wrong guesses and instances of foresight.

The depressing thing is, however, that people seem quick to ascribe powers of foresight to people who predict things accurately, even if they have predicted lots of other things inaccurately. Astrologers and pundits alike point to past successful predictions as evidence that they possess a foresight denied to the rest of us.

If you find yourself in control of a largish group, here's something you can do. Ask everyone to stand up, concentrate hard and try to predict whether a coin you toss will be heads or tails. Toss it, announce the result, and ask all those who got it wrong to sit down. Repeat until just one or two people are standing. Well done – you've found your psychics! I've done this with groups of 50–100, and what happens is that someone gets it right several times in a row, as random luck would predict. Psychic powers are not needed to explain the result. This often feels uncanny to the people guessing correctly. It's as though we can't help but believe correct guesses are indicative of some kind of mysterious foresight.

See also

42. The lady doth protest too much

Motivation speculation

> That Darwinist authorities find public scrutiny of their theory so threatening indicates to me that there is a hidden insecurity in their intellectual position which will eventually become so visible it can no longer be concealed.
>
> Phillip E. Johnson, Intelligent Design theorist[59]

Despite philosophical difficulties concerning how we know other people have minds at all, in everyday life we are actually pretty good at knowing the mental states of others. Most of us find feelings of boredom, irritation or attraction very hard to conceal, and often it takes just one look to detect someone's mood.

However, one of Freud's more regrettable legacies is that he seems to have convinced a large number of us that we are better judges of others' minds than those concerned are themselves. Our subconscious may be hidden from us, but apparently it seems transparent to others.

There is a set of crass pop-psychology rules for making these sweeping judgements about people's true motivations. One is the inverse-proportion denial rule – otherwise known as 'The Lady Doth Protest Too Much manoeuvre' – which states that the more someone denies something the more likely it is to be true. As every schoolboy thinks he knows, someone who makes a big point of denying he is gay, for example, is probably gay himself.

Another related rule is the hatred-equals-fear rule – otherwise known as the scared bigot response. This states that the more someone professes to hate something, the more likely she is to actually be afraid of it. The ability to apply this rule is not usually mastered until we become self-righteous undergraduates.

Then there is the arrogance as insecurity rule, otherwise known as the soft-centre principle. This states that anyone who seems to be excessively confident is almost certainly compensating for a deep-rooted insecurity. The main beneficiaries of this are arrogant, predatory men.

The trouble with all these pseudo-rules is that they are all baloney. Of course, there are specific instances when a person who aggressively denies his homosexuality, claims to hate 'poofs' and acts more macho than Ernest Hemingway at a bachelor party, really is struggling to come to terms with his own sexual feelings for other men. But it might equally be the case that he's just a bigoted, macho homophobe. Most people protest that something is not true because they really think it isn't true, and the truth in this instance matters to them. I hate Earl Grey tea, but I'm not afraid of it. And some people are arrogant precisely because they're not insecure about anything.

So much should be evident. And yet we still find people who in so-called intellectual discussions invoke just these kinds of crass psychological generalizations to support their case. Creation scientist Phillip Johnson's swipe against the

'Darwinist authorities' is one example. He very cleverly describes their resistance to people such as himself in terms of their being 'threatened', which is already to imply their reaction is not an intellectual but a defensive, psychological one. He then suggests that the vociferous nature of their defence against creation scientists is due to some 'hidden insecurity in their reasoning', thus treating rational arguments in psychoanalytic terms.

If we were to apply this kind of analysis to the analyst, we might suggest that Johnson is so fixed in the rightness (and righteousness) of his own position that he cannot comprehend that people might object to him on good intellectual and scientific grounds rather than emotional ones. That may well be true, but it might equally well not be. If we want to criticize him, we should just point out that his attempt to play the analyst is trite and completely fails to address any of the serious issues at stake. Speculating as to what subconscious psychological desire or hidden intellectual insecurity motivated him to do so may be good fun and tremendously interesting, but it is both futile and irrelevant to judging the soundness of his case.

Since we all seem to be amateur psychoanalysts now, perhaps we owe it to ourselves to check how subtly or crassly we apply our craft. See how often you are tempted to speculate as to the hidden psychological motivations for people's actions and beliefs, and then ask yourself if you really have decent justifications for these speculations. You might learn something about yourself.

See also

43. Fighting crime with concerts

Correlation is not causation

> The arts have their value in society. You look at the Royal
> Albert Hall on Proms night. How many of those people are
> going to mug old ladies on the way home? Not many –
> they've got more important things to worry about.
>
> Prunella Scales, actor[60]

It is indeed highly unlikely that anyone returning from a classical music concert is going to mug someone along the way. But
such a person is also probably more likely than the average
member of the population to embezzle funds from their company the day after. Are we then to conclude that listening to
Mozart will make you less likely to mug someone but more
likely to fiddle the books?

The conclusion would seem at best premature and at worst
simply absurd. The problem is a straightforward confusion of
correlations and causes.

For example, Britons who regularly eat plantains are also
more likely to regularly eat yams. Does that mean eating one
causes people to eat the other? Of course not. The explanation
of the correlation is a third factor: plantains and yams are both
staples of the Caribbean diet. Coming from a family of
Caribbean origin is thus the causal factor which explains the
correlation between consumption of both foodstuffs.

Similarly, it remains true that audiences at classical music concerts tend to be middle class, a social group not prone to mugging but with a virtual monopoly on corporate fraud. It is far more likely that these broader facts about social position do more to explain the lack of muggers in Prom audiences than any morally improving quality in the music.

Even if, as a matter of fact, the music does affect its listeners' morality, the important point is that the mere correlation of reduced criminality and listening to orchestras does not show that it does.

The existence of a correlation can suggest that there might be a causal story to be told that links the two, as is the case with both my examples. But often there is little to be gained by telling it. The setting of the sun may explain both the closing of a flower and the locking of the park gates by the keeper, but the two effects are still caused by two very different mechanisms and have no deep connection. Similarly, the nine o'clock train leaves at the same time as the nine o'clock radio news bulletin starts. (Well, perhaps not on Britain's railways.) But to say that both are caused by it being nine o'clock is surely an error: times are just the wrong kind of thing to be causes. The mere sharing of a common causal factor does not provide a causal link between two such events.

Leaping from correlation to cause does seem to come naturally to us, perhaps because, as David Hume argued[61], regular correlations of a certain sort are ultimately the only evidence that there is such a thing as causation at all. (Many claim he went further and argued that causation was just a form of exceptionless correlation.) But even Hume would agree that it's not just any correlation that points to a cause.

News pages are full of reports of correlations where it is implied that there is some causal link. Consider, for example, what causal links might be assumed from the following findings, all reported in the British media: truants are more than five times as likely to take drugs as other schoolchildren; Gulf War veterans are twice as likely as other servicemen and women to report ill health; black people are six times more likely to be sent to prison than whites. You can see how easy it would be to infer certain causal links from these correlations, but what other, possibly better, explanations for the links are there?

See also

44. What right have you got?

Playing the rights card

> What right do we have to touch and smell an animal that
> has rested beneath the surface for 10,000 years?
>
> David G. Anderson, anthropologist[62]

The UN's Universal Declaration of Human Rights has become a quasi-sacred document, the benchmark against which the decency of a country is measured. Human Rights NGOs such as Amnesty International are virtually beyond criticism, for what they are defending is so obviously just. Democratic governments pass laws at their peril that are perceived to infringe on the 'inalienable' rights of their citizens.

The discourse of rights is extremely powerful in the public domain. But intellectually speaking, rights command less than universal respect. Philosopher and social reformer Jeremy Bentham famously said that talk of 'natural rights is simple nonsense: natural and imprescriptible rights, rhetorical nonsense – nonsense upon stilts'. Many since have broadly agreed, arguing that rights are not the moral basis of law, but products of the law, which has its moral basis in something completely different.

Whether one takes the broadly Benthamite line or not, what is clear and obvious is that it is not clear or obvious what rights are, where they come from, and which rights we really have. What is the right to life and what kinds of beings have it?

Does the right to work entail a duty on the part of the state to provide work? Does the right to free speech include hate speech? Yet such complexities are often swept away by the rhetoric of 'playing the rights card'.

One powerful way to do this is to ask 'What right do you have to . . . ?' It puts the person questioned on the back foot and seems to demand an answer. But must we give one? In general, we do not require specific rights to perform specific actions. Someone who challenged us to state by which right we whistled, used the toilet or read a newspaper on a train would be asking a very odd question indeed. We generally have the right to do whatever we want, as long as we don't break the law or infringe on other people's rights of non-interference.

As part of his argumentative armoury, the anthropologist David G. Anderson asked a rhetorical question about what right we have to dig up a mammoth's remains. The question came in the context of a piece detailing the interesting traditions, rituals and – though he might find the word too judgemental – myths of the Evenki, a people indigenous to Siberia. He pointed out the conflicts between the scientists who want to get their hands on mammoth remains and the Evenki, who allow such remains to be taken only if they 'present themselves'. Even then, a gift must be left in return.

There may be reasons for not digging up the mammoth remains – such as respect or the desire not to offend – but it is not incumbent on those who do dig them up to show by what right they do so. To say that the dead mammoth has a right not to be disturbed is surely stretching the notion of rights too far. Nor is it the case that the Evenki have an inalienable right not to be offended. As John Stuart Mill persuasively argued, if that were the case we'd have to ban anything that anyone took offence at. The only right we need is the legal one to dig on the land and take away what we find.

Just as it can be rhetorically powerful to demand erroneously by which right people act, so it can be effective to claim a right as justifying one's own action. Yet when people claim the government owes them support to conceive a child artificially because they have a right to have children, that they should be allowed to spread racist or homophobic views because they have a right to free speech, or even that there is no need for greater gun controls in America because of the right to bear arms, it should be clear that it is all too easy to invoke a seemingly unobjectionable right to justify a controversial course of action.

How right are you about rights? Do you have a right to a job? If so, does someone else have a duty to make sure your right can be exercised? Does your right to your opinion extend to a right to have it heard? Do you support the rights of refugees to claim sanctuary in your country? Which rights do you think have concomitant duties?

See also

45. It didn't work then, so . . .

Faulty induction

> Crime and terror would be better addressed with 10,000 more police and a national border force, rather than wasting £3 billion on ID cards that didn't protect people in the US or Spain and which would curtail British rights and liberties.
>
> Matthew Taylor, chairman of the Liberal Democrats[63]

Bertrand Russell once told a story about the turkey who, noting that he had always been fed at sunrise, concluded that 'I am always fed at sunrise' held as a general rule. On Christmas morning it therefore came as a bit of shock when, instead of getting feed down his neck, he got his neck wrung.

The moral of the story is that, although we have no choice but to base our expectations of the future on the experience of history, past performance is no guarantee of future returns.

Just how we do reliably infer facts about the present and future from the past is the 'problem of induction', and it has bothered philosophers for centuries. But although the deep philosophical issues remain unresolved, we have some idea what, for practical purposes, counts as drawing an unwarranted conclusion from the past.

Matthew Taylor's objection to ID cards counts as one such unjustified inference. He pointed out that ID cards failed to stop terrorist attacks in New York and Madrid, concluding that the money the scheme requires would serve security and crime-fighting better if it were spent on 'more police and a national border force'.

As an argument this is no better than the old 'My grand-mother smoked twenty cigarettes a day and lived to 101' chestnut. So what? No one says that if you smoke you will definitely die because of your habit. The claim is only that it massively increases your chances of an early death, and no individual chain-smoking centenarian can make that claim untrue. Similarly, there are lots of ways you can increase your chances of living longer, and the case of someone who didn't smoke, drank little, exercised every day and wasn't overweight but dropped dead of a heart attack aged thirty-two doesn't change these general facts.

On 9/11, of course New Yorkers weren't protected by compulsory ID cards, because the US doesn't have them. In Madrid, they didn't stop a terrorist attack. But not even their most passionate advocates claim that ID cards are a foolproof prophylactic against terrorism. Like the healthy man who drops dead, the ID-carrying Spaniards who were killed on 9 March 2004 prove nothing about the contribution identification might make to security.

The error of thinking it does is compounded when you consider that we are not even comparing like with like. Britain's system might work where Spain's did not because it would be significantly different.

Several things can help create a gaping chasm between 'it didn't work there and then' to 'it won't work here and now'. One is that the 'it' may not be the same – or at least sufficiently similar – in both cases. A second is that the circumstances of here and now may differ in relevant respects from those of there and then. A third is that a measure which is designed to increase or decrease the likelihood of something happening can 'work', even if on a particular occasion it didn't stop or cause that thing to happen. Defibrillators work even though they have failed to save some people's lives.

Nevertheless, are we not obliged to draw on experience of the past in some way in order to learn for the future? It may be true that nothing follows directly from events in Spain, but shouldn't their experience inform the UK debate? Well, yes. The trick is to apportion weight to past experience proportionately to the relevance it has for the present circumstances. Even when nothing strictly follows from what happened in the past, we would be foolish to forget about it altogether.

Consider some difficult cases of where what it is possible to learn form other places or times is not clear. How much can America learn from the Scandinavian social model, when the two cultures are very different? Does the behaviour of our ancestors in the Pleistocene really tell us anything about human nature now? Would the occupation of Iraq by the USA and its allies have been more successful if the generals and politicians had studied Iraqi history?

See also

46. God is an alien

Logically consistent nonsense

The Gods were not metaphysical beings born of human-
ity's overactive imagination, but extraterrestrials who left
traces of their presence everywhere on Earth.

Erich von Däniken, author of *Chariots of the Gods?*[64]

As a teenager, I read Erich von Däniken's *Chariots of the Gods?*
with intense fascination. Its astonishing hypothesis was that, in
ancient times, aliens visited the earth, left behind artefacts and
interbred with us. The Nazca lines in Peru were, he claimed,
landing strips for spacecraft, while the intervention of aliens
explains otherwise incredible feats of engineering such as
Stonehenge and the great pyramids. Stories of gods coming
from the skies are not ancient myths, but literal tales of visiting
extraterrestrials.

Von Däniken's twenty-six books have sold more than 60
million copies. His theories, however, are not taken seriously in
academic places of learning: his case is just too flimsy. Why
then do they seem so persuasive to so many lay readers?

Von Däniken's theory has two features which make it convincing, despite the weakness of the evidence for it. The first is
that the theory largely fits the facts. You might think this would
recommend it, but actually any number of cranky theories can
fit the facts. For example, the theory that Google is planning to

take control of all the world's data fits many known facts: they have got many people to give them their personal data; they dominate web search; their googledocs utility not only stores millions of files, its terms and conditions actually give Google 'a worldwide, non-exclusive, royalty-free licence to reproduce, adapt, modify, publish and distribute such content on Google services for the purpose of displaying, distributing and promoting Google services'. Spooky, huh?

The problem is that fitting the facts is not the same as best explaining the facts. If my cat disappears, the theory that the cat is the feline messiah and has ascended to Kitty Heaven fits this fact, but it is not the best explanation of it. However, we are easily impressed when an explanation seems to fit many facts, as von Däniken's undoubtedly does.

Second, von Däniken's view is internally consistent. He works out his theory with admirable thoroughness, so that all parts of it fit together in a coherent way. Like fitting the facts, this is again usually thought of as a recommendation for a theory, but being logically consistent is only a minimal requirement for a theory to be taken seriously. A good one has to do more than this: it needs to explain the phenomenon under scrutiny better than competing theories. But the idea that alien visitations propelled our evolution, biologically and culturally, is more extravagant, more speculative, and creates more new questions than the rival hypothesis that we've just been bumbling along all by ourselves.

Sometimes, a logically consistent theory which fits the facts is suspicious because it explains too much. There are all sorts of holes in the official version of the JFK assassination, for example. But many conspiracy theories promise to explain everything. Far from being a sign of their credibility, this may indicate just the opposite: loose ends are often to be expected if we confine ourselves to what is known.

We should learn to be less impressed by mere consistency. Best explanations are not only coherent, they are testable; they have predictive power; and they fit not just the facts of the case but other known facts as well.

Theodicies are attempts to reconcile the existence of great horrors and suffering in the world with the existence of an all-powerful, all-loving God. I think they do often succeed in showing there is no logical contradiction between the two things. But don't they fail to meet all the other criteria for a sound theory? You cannot test them. Their predictive and explanatory powers are weak, since no one who believes in a good God would really expect him to allow torture, gang rape, tsunamis or flesh-eating diseases. And don't the known facts about how many awful things happen on earth better fit the explanation that God either doesn't exist or doesn't care? Could it be that the good God hypothesis is the most egregious example of logically consistent nonsense we have?

See also

47. That old chestnut

Argumentum ad fatigum

> I don't accept the premise that he didn't have weapons of mass destruction . . . He certainly had the capability, he had the intention to go on developing the programmes, and he very certainly contravened the Security Council resolutions on that. So I don't think we need to rake over that old ground.

> Sir Jeremy Greenstock, Her Majesty's former special representative in Iraq[65]

Country is truly the music of philosophers, and Kenny Rogers surely ranks among its Platos. In 'The Gambler' Rogers says you've got to 'Know when to walk away and know when to run.' But when it comes to a rational argument, it's very hard to judge when the time to quit is right.

Part of the problem is what might be called *argumentum ad fatigum*. This is where debates are won, or at least positions relinquished, solely because people have been worn down. If you hear a bad argument often enough, you might just end up thinking it's not so bad after all. Likewise, if you reject a good argument enough times, people will end up believing there must be something to the refutation.

The power of persistence was given a comic example by Eddie Murphy in one of his stand-up routines. Murphy described a man who was seen by his girlfriend leaving another woman's house. When confronted with this, all he did was simply keep repeating 'It wasn't me.' After a while, the woman seriously doubted whether she had really seen him in the first place. It's a grotesque exaggeration but, unfortunately, there is something in it. Psychology experiments show that if the majority of a group falsely claim that the shortest of two lines is actually the longest, others will probably believe them rather than the evidence of their own senses.

Such is the power of the *argumentum ad fatigum* that sometimes you need only to refer to the old age of the discussion to achieve your effect. 'Do we have to go over this again?' you might ask. The answer might be 'yes', because previous discussions were inconclusive. But still, the person coming back to the problem is made to feel that it's they who are being tiresome or getting it all wrong, rather than the person who is refusing to engage.

Sir Jeremy Greenstock, Her Majesty's former special representative in Iraq did this when asked about the claims that Saddam Hussein had WMD. At a time when the British government had not yet admitted its intelligence was wrong and a war was being fought that was still premised partly on the WMD claim, his relegation of the dispute to 'old ground' was extraordinary.

Resisting the *argumentum ad fatigum* move requires standing up to the intimidation it implies. Just calmly reply that the issue may be old but, since no satisfactory answer has yet been given, it is still very much alive.

That old chestnut

It's hard to be really honest about when we are simply fed up with arguing and when all that can usefully be said has been said. Do creationists not understand that evolution is not 'just one theory among many' or are they making points evolutionists have not given satisfactory answers to? Are the questions asked about the Warren Report any less unanswered just because the people who keep asking them are labelled cranky conspiracy theorists who won't give up? Have the allegations that George W. Bush stole the 2000 presidential election been refuted or merely battered into submission? What has been exhausted – the arguments or you?

See also

48. They would say that

Immunization against error

Romantic love has taken precedence over all other relationships, probably because it offers an escape from reality. It's a complete con, of course, because it doesn't last, and anyone who says it does is lying.

Emma Thompson, actor[66]

Since its birth in Ancient Greece, philosophy has sought the holy grail of certain knowledge. Philosophy has often reflected a common human desire to have things clear-cut. This desire can be satisfied – psychologically, if not logically – through the adoption of beliefs which are immunized against the very possibility of error.

Thompson's assertion about romantic love is a typical example. She believes that it never lasts. The problem is, of course, that some people claim it does. If, however, Thompson adopts the maxim 'People who tell you romantic love lasts are lying,' then no such avowals count as evidence against her. If you agree you add support to her thesis, but if you disagree, that simply shows you are a liar, and this also fits her thesis. Heads Thompson wins, tails you lose.

If you are as convinced as Thompson seems to be, any apparent counter-example can be explained away. Lifelong partners Adam and Steve may act and talk as though they were still in love, but Thompson could always maintain that deep down they are not, or that what they call 'love' isn't really romantic love. (Thompson may be right that romantic love doesn't last, by the way. It's the way her theory rules out possible counter-evidence that bothers me.)

Traditionally, this kind of claim would be called unfalsifiable, meaning that nothing would count as evidence for its falsity. Jean-Paul Sartre seemed to make a similarly unfalsifiable claim when he claimed that we all feel anguish, and the reason why some people don't appear to be anguished is because 'they are merely disguising their anguish or are in flight from it'. What that means is that no one can be held up as a counter-example to the thesis. A lack of apparent anguish can always be explained away as the result of disguise or flight.

People usually don't make unfalsifiable claims in order consciously to immunize themselves against error. On the contrary, the popularity of such assertions is precisely their apparent certainty. The fact that no evidence exists to counter a thesis is usually a good reason to suppose it is true. But sometimes we fail to notice that the lack of counter-evidence is due to the fact that its very possibility is ruled out by the claim being made. It is like a court case where the only admissible witnesses are those who support the prosecution. In such a rigged trial, it is not surprising that all the evidence falls on one side.

Immunization against error is most evident in conspiracy theories, since any apparent counter-evidence can be viewed as evidence of the effectiveness of the conspiracy. The official 9/11 Commission, for instance, is seen as part of the conspiracy, and so all the evidence it presented can just be dismissed. 'They would say that,' is how apparent counter-evidence is rebutted.

Even if we are not attracted to conspiracy theories, such

ways of thinking are quite common. I have met Christians who refuse to accept the evidence that non-believers have fulfilled lives, because they take it as a foundational belief that everyone deep down suffers from separation from Christ, whether they know it or not. Likewise, many atheists refuse to accept the apparent reasonableness of many believers on the grounds that anyone who is religious must be suffering from an irrational delusion. It seems that we can't help trying to immunize our most cherished beliefs against error. If you say you don't, it's my bet you're lying, stupid or in denial. *Touché*.

Have you never, in an immune system-like response, repelled a view that contradicts your own with a 'they would say that'? One of the most searching questions we can ask ourselves is: what would make me revise my most firmly held belief? If you cannot think of a realistic piece of evidence that would do this for you, the chances are you have become too fixed in you opinion to even countenance the possibility that it might be wrong.

See also

49. That way lies disaster

Slippery slopes

It is the beginning of a very long and slippery slope and none of us can say where it would end up.

Robert Hazell, professor of government[67]

For decades now British politics has been grappling with the 'West Lothian question': with power devolved to Scotland, Wales or Northern Ireland, members of parliament from those regions still vote on matters that solely concern the English. Yet MPs from English constituencies have no say on those matters in the other countries of the United Kingdom. Since Tam Dalyell first put the question in 1977, more powers have been devolved to the national assemblies, but England remains solely under the control of the UK parliament. It's all very messy and inconsistent.

One solution seems simple and obvious: when Parliament considers legislation which solely pertains to England, then only English MPs should be entitled to vote. In effect this creates a parliament within parliament – an English one within the British.

Professor Robert Hazell, director of the constitution unit at University College London, thinks this is a bad idea for several reasons. One of these is that it would be 'the beginning of a very long and slippery slope'.

The problem with slippery slope arguments is that they blur the focus on what is contentious. In the West Lothian Question case, we need to ask: would it be a bad thing in itself to have a parliament within a parliament, or would that be a problem only if this led to the further fragmenting of the United Kingdom? Invoking a slippery slope argument can be a way of avoiding the first question.

In general terms, instead of focusing on the actual wrongness of the action under debate, slippery slope arguments shift our focus to its unacceptable extensions. In this way they can avert our attention from what is really at issue and make us look elsewhere. This is often the case when discussing new medical technologies. Instead of asking whether it is morally acceptable to create a human clone, for example, the debate turns to what other things might happen if we start down this road. Often these are outlandish fears, for example, of dictators creating thousands of copies of themselves. But even if the scenarios imagined are more plausible, arguing this way doesn't actually tell us what we urgently need to know, that is, whether creating human clones is right in itself.

A slippery slope argument can carry some weight if there is a high probability that the unacceptable consequence will in fact happen, and is actually unacceptable. Hazell knows his constitutional history, and when he says a parliament within a parliament risks taking us further down the road to disintegration of the UK than we would want, he should be listened to. The problem is that in most slippery slope arguments, no sober assessment about the likelihood of falling down it is given.

Another major problem with slippery slope arguments is that they tend to underestimate the extent to which slopes can be made less greasy. By invoking a sense of inevitability, they encourage us to be more fatalistic than we perhaps should be. For instance, legalizing abortion has not set us on a slippery slope towards infanticide. In fact, in the UK and the US, most of the pressure is now coming to bring down the number of weeks up to which an embryo can legally be aborted.

When confronted with a slippery slope argument, two questions should be asked. First, is the practice being objected to in itself objectionable? If it is, then the foreseen extensions are irrelevant. If the practice is not objectionable in itself, we then need to ask, if we start down this road, is it likely that the practice would be extended to situations where it was objectionable? Only if it is will the slippery slope argument carry any force. And even then, that may only provide reasons for creating safeguards to prevent the unwanted extension.

How slippery are many of the slopes we are constantly warned about? Does permissiveness about soft drugs really lead to acceptance of harder ones? Do the restrictions on liberty defended as necessary in the war on terror risk undermining the essential freedoms of Western democracies? Would allowing genetic enhancements *in utero* inevitably lead to a future in which society would be divided between genetic haves and have-nots?

See also

50. Not so sound bites

Vacuous pseudo-wisdom

> The poor sell drugs so they can buy Nikes and the rich sell
> Nikes so they can buy drugs.

Frédéric Beigbeder, £9.99 [68]

It is widely lamented in serious circles that we live in the age of
the soundbite. Nuanced arguments have been replaced with
rapid-fire rhetoric for the zero attention span generation. The
short, sharp, memorable phrase is king.

'Soundbite', however, is more a term of abuse than a factual
description. If you approve of what is said pithily and memo-
rably, all of a sudden it is not a soundbite after all, but an
aphorism or a 'pearl of wisdom'. Quotations lifted from literature, film or theatre are often dignified in this way. In order to
emphasize their shared features with soundbites, let us call them
'wisebites'.

What is ironic is that the very people who often scorn the
soundbite for its shallowness often fall for a wisebite which is
equally vacuous, if not more so. Take, for instance, the quotation
above from Frédéric Beigbeder's novel *£9.99*. One reviewer of
the book singled it out as an example of the writer's brilliant
ability to hit the nail on the head. But the wisebite falls apart at
the slightest examination. It just isn't true.

Of course some poor people sell drugs in order to afford

more consumer goods, and some people who work for multi-nationals are drug-takers. But the wisebite implies much more than this – that there is a kind of vicious circle of consumption: the rich create a need or desire for the poor to acquire consumer goods so that they themselves can fund their drug habits, which are in turn supplied by the poor. Capitalism is thus a kind of self-perpetuating mechanism for keeping the poor poor and the rich stoned. This is hardly a nuanced or insightful description of the true, complex relations between drug users and suppliers, multinationals and the poor.

Is it even true that the poor generally sell drugs? Drug dealers are often from poor backgrounds but they themselves are often very wealthy indeed. Many of their drugs are in fact sold to the poor, whose addiction keeps them in penury. But then the idea that the ex-poor are exploiting the still-poor doesn't appeal to the intellectual classes as much as the idea that the poor are victims of greedy corporations.

Strip away the nonsense from the wisebite, then, and you are left with the truism that the poor aspire to acquire material goods and this desire is partly fuelled by the producers of these goods. Furthermore, some rich people take drugs. That really does not leave much of the original sentiment intact.

Compare this with a bona fide soundbite. Former British premier Tony Blair was fond of saying 'No rights without responsibilities'. The soundbite is too simplistic. Newborn infants, for instance, have rights without responsibilities. But take away the obvious exceptions and at least there is a serious point being made. If we are to have rights in a society then certainly people have responsibilities to uphold them or not to infringe them. The general existence of rights does entail concomitant responsibilities.

In this battle of the bites, it is thus the derided soundbite which emerges the stronger and the celebrated wisebite turns out to be hollow. It seems we are as ready to be beguiled by the false but wise-sounding 'aphorisms' of the writer, poet or intellectual as we are to dismiss the soundbites of the politician. Their relative merits rarely come into play.

How many wise old sayings really are wise? Consider some of the most enduring: 'The unexamined life is not worth living,' 'Without God, anything is permitted,' 'Better safe than sorry.' Are these genuine insights or just soundbites that have stuck?

See also

51. Meet Mr Loophole

Legality and morality

> I did nothing wrong. I broke no laws. I broke no rules of the House.
>
> Congressman Tom DeLay[69]

In 2005 a Texas grand jury indicted the Republican congressman Tom DeLay for conspiring to violate Texas state election laws concerning the funding of political campaigns. DeLay denied the charges, saying they were politically motivated: the campaign finance investigation was led by Travis County, Texas District Attorney Ronnie Earle, a Democrat. DeLay, a former House majority leader, did not seek re-election in 2006 and at the time of writing was still awaiting trial.

Did DeLay do anything wrong? In one sense it is of course too soon to say: we must await the result of his trial. But will that actually settle matters? That depends on which question you are asking. Were DeLay's statements quoted above three separate claims, or three parts of one claim?

They should be three. The first, 'I did nothing wrong,' is a moral claim. Morality and legality are two different matters. Sometimes what is illegal is nonetheless right, such as when Rosa Parks disobeyed Montgomery's racial segregation laws and sat in a seat reserved for white people. This is the flipside of the fact that what is legal is sometimes nonetheless wrong, such as discriminating according to race in the first place.

So when DeLay said 'I broke no laws,' this is a different claim from the one that he did nothing wrong. Similarly, 'I broke no rules of the House' is a third claim, since Congress regulates itself and to break its rules may on occasion be neither immoral nor illegal.

I can't read DeLay's mind, and perhaps he meant to make three separate claims, and I'm sure he would defend all three propositions individually. But there are other plausible readings of his statement which do not see the three elements as being so distinct. Many people hearing him talk would have assumed that the assertions that he broke no rules or laws are what justified his first claim that he did no wrong. The quote, from a television interview, could have been transcribed as 'I did nothing wrong: I broke no laws, I broke no rules of the House.' People often say something like this when they invoke rules and laws in their moral defence. It is not, however, a sound way of reasoning.

The most cynical way of viewing this common manoeuvre is that people try to hide behind the law. Some are more honest and drop any pretence that a legal defence is a moral one. In the UK, the lawyer Nick Freeman has become something of a celebrity and earned the title 'Mr Loophole' for his success in overturning driving convictions for his often wealthy clients. Freeman does not even pretend to claim that none of his clients did anything wrong. Of one of the drink-driving convictions he helped overturn, he said, 'There was no doubt the driver was over the limit.'[70] If that client were to claim that they did nothing wrong, and their legal innocence proves this, their argument would be unsound.

More charitably, going to the courts is sometimes the only robust way to refute a public claim of wrongdoing. For instance, the author of *The Da Vinci Code*, Dan Brown, was sued by two of the authors of *The Holy Blood and the Holy Grail* for plagiarizing their work. They lost their case. It is strictly accurate to say that Brown may have done nothing legally wrong but that doesn't mean he did nothing morally wrong, but since Brown has successfully defended himself using the only means available to him, you would need good reasons to justify continuing to cast the shadow of doubt upon him. Sometimes, when deciding if someone is right or wrong, the law is all we have to go on.

When is it reasonable to separate law and morality as they logically should be? Is it fair to insist that the acquitted OJ Simpson did wrong? What about Rabei Osman, the Egyptian accused of being the mastermind of the Madrid bombings, who also walked free from court? Or British National Party leader Nick Griffin, cleared of inciting racial hatred? Legal innocence may not entail moral innocence, but in public life at least, must we sometimes use the former as a proxy for the latter?

See also

52. Single-parent slurs

Failing to disaggregate

The professional literature of criminology is surprisingly consistent on the real root causes of violent crime: the breakdown of the family and community stability. The sequence has its deepest roots in the absence of stable marriage.

Patrick F. Fagan, 'The Real Root Causes of Violent Crime'[71]

Those who are socially conservative frequently argue that the evidence that 'marriage works' is incontrovertible. But although there is no reason to doubt the accuracy of the statistics people like Patrick F. Fagan cite, their case is flawed because it fails to take into account what statisticians call disaggregation: the breaking down of statistics into their component parts.

Statistics do indeed regularly indicate a correlation between marriage and various goods, both social and personal. Similarly, divorce and single-parenthood are correlated with various ills. Children of unmarried parents are more likely to take drugs, turn to crime, drop out of university, get divorced themselves, and experience virtually every other nasty thing you'd never want your children to go through.

The trouble with most of the surveys that produce these results is that they deal only with very broad categories: the married, cohabitees, divorcees, single parents. This means their findings would be consistent with a hypothesis contrary to that espoused by Fagan: that it is not marriage per se which is good for people, but long-term committed relationships. We would expect to find more of these kinds of relationships in the married group than the cohabiting group, simply because all marriages are at least in theory long-term commitments (whether they are fulfilled or not), whereas cohabitations need not be. It is therefore more than possible that marriage is not a prerequisite for the social benefits Fagan values after all, but is merely the most common social sign that the commitment required to achieve these values is present in a relationship.

Indeed, Fagan's own detailed results are fully consistent with this interpretation. The initial factors which he says lead to juvenile crime are paternal absence, absence of maternal love, parental fighting, lack of parental supervision and discipline, rejection of the child, parental abuse or neglect, and criminal parents. It should be obvious that none of these factors is linked by necessity to the marital status of the parents. Cohabitees can avoid all of these failings and married couples can exhibit most of them.

It is important to realize that this is not just a problem caused by the fact that statistics always need to be interpreted. Interpretation would be much easier if we were able to distinguish between people cohabiting with no commitment to the future, right through to those who have spent a lifetime together without exchanging wedding vows. If we looked at the married, we would find, as well as strong, stable relationships, domestic disasters which are bad for both spouses. Then we would be better placed to judge whether marriage really is a crucial factor, or whether it's simply a matter of commitment, or something else.

We are constantly bombarded with statistics that have not been disaggregated, and as a result, it is very hard to know exactly what they mean. The key to not being duped is always to ask yourself how people have been divided up for each survey, and whether this glosses over other possibly more illuminating distinctions.

Would disaggregation answer the following questions? Do vegetarians live longer because they're vegetarians, or because they're generally more health conscious than everyone else lumped together as carnivores? Does the fact that they are faith-based explain why some church schools often produce better results, or do you need to look at the social backgrounds of their intake? Are people with philosophy degrees more likely than others to be unemployed six months after graduation because they studied philosophy, or because the subject attracts layabouts?

See also

53. Safe, in no uncertain terms

The precautionary principle

> The precautionary principle means that, if you are unsure of what the result will be, especially if it is going to be so serious, it would be wiser not to do it until more evidence is available.
>
> Royal Society for the Protection of Birds spokesperson[72]

The precautionary principle is appealed to in all sorts of contexts, as though it were a straightforward, obvious idea we can all understand and use. In fact, the principle is used in a myriad of ways, some of them vague and misleading.

In the example above, the principle is taken to mean: do not do anything where the outcome is uncertain and potentially serious until more evidence is available. The obvious problem here is that the outcome of almost all actions is uncertain, and often potentially serious. Even a simple decision like driving a long distance has an uncertain, potentially fatal outcome. (In the UK, road accidents are the most common cause of death among the under thirty-fives.) Are we then not to drive 'until more evidence is available'?

Obviously this is absurd. What we need is *enough* evidence to make an informed choice, which we do in the case of driving. In contrast, the version of the principle above was invoked in the context of a discussion about genetically modified crops.

In the RSPB's view, 'Insufficient laboratory tests have been done on the effect of GM crops before going to field-scale trials.' Strictly speaking then, the principle should read: Do not do anything where the outcome is uncertain and potentially serious until enough evidence is available to make an informed choice.

The key question now becomes, 'What is enough evidence?' A credible answer is 'That which is sufficient to conduct a proper risk assessment.' Risk assessment is about weighing the desirability of outcomes against the risks involved in the actions required to achieve these outcomes. We can now state the precautionary principle in a coherent way: do not proceed in a course of action with potentially serious consequences until you have conducted a proper risk analysis based on sufficient evidence. This captures the spirit of what the RSPB spokesperson was trying to say.

This makes it clear that the precautionary principle needs to be employed in tandem with risk assessment. It does not amount to the claim that the existence of risk or uncertainty in themselves provides a reason for not acting. Risk analysis is about dealing with uncertainty – where there is certainty there is no risk. The principle is thus not a kind of blanket policy of risk-aversion. This is just as well, because if the precautionary principle just amounted to saying 'do not take unnecessarily large risks' it would be a mere platitude.

The RSPB's rather vaguer formulation is, unfortunately, closer to the one which is most often used. Consider this pair of definitions of the precautionary principle offered by newspapers:

'You should not adopt any new technology unless you are certain it is safe.'[73]

'Nothing should ever be done until it has been proved safe.'[74]

These demands are too high. With proof and certainty, there would be no risk, but, as we've seen, the precautionary principle cannot be about avoiding risk altogether. And because what these versions of the precautionary principle ask us to prove is so hard to establish – that no harm is done – meeting their criteria becomes impossible.

Look at how the idea of the precautionary principle is actually used and more often than not, I would wager, you'll see it is used in this defective sense. The misuse of the principle is objectionable mostly because it encourages people to ignore the fact that we constantly have to make decisions based on incomplete knowledge and a judgement of risk. Instead, it offers the illusion that we can avoid doing things which are not certain to be safe.

What do you make of the following invocations of the precautionary principle? British security services have invoked it to appeal for powers to raise the number of days a terror suspect can be detained without charge from twenty-eight to fifty-six days. The Nobel Peace Prize committee, in their citation for Al Gore's award, used it to underline the importance of action on climate change. A report from Europol and the European Monitoring Centre for Drugs and Drug Addiction used the principle to support its calls for a ban of the legal dance drug BZP. Sensible precautions all, or excessive risk-aversion?

See also

54. The weapons they couldn't find

Absence and evidence

> You see, the International Atomic Agency has gone in and done an exhaustive survey, inspections of these sites. And while they say we can't disprove the rumours, the allegations that Iran is pursuing secret programs, we have no evidence to sustain any allegation or speculation that Iran is – how do you prove a negative?
>
> Scott Ritter, former UN weapons inspector in Iran[75]

In recent years, many commentators have argued that the United States is going to do with Iran what it did with Iraq. After the UN weapons inspections in Iraq, history seemed to be repeating itself with the International Atomic Energy Agency (IAEA) inspections in Iran. UN inspectors were, it is said, set the hopeless task of proving a negative: that Saddam Hussein did not have weapons of mass destruction. Because this could not be done, the US and its allies would never have the evidence they demanded to avert an invasion. Likewise, the IAEA had to prove that Iran did not have a nuclear weapons programme, and since you couldn't prove that negative either, America would get another pretext to launch military strikes.

Former UN weapons inspector Scott Ritter expressed his scepticism of the IAEA's task by asking 'How do you prove a negative?' The implied answer to this rhetorical question is 'You can't.' But look at how Ritter continued: 'And the concern of Iran is that when you look at the Iraq model, the United States pressured the Security Council of the United Nations to make the same demands on Saddam Hussein. Saddam must prove he does not have weapons of mass destruction programs. It turns out that Saddam had terminated them in 1991, and there were no programs there, but nothing the Iraqi regime could do would satisfy the American demands.'

There is something very odd about this reply. Ritter's main point is how unreasonable it is to ask someone to prove a negative. And yet he says clearly, 'Saddam had terminated' his WMD programme in 1991. So Ritter himself accepts as proven at least one negative: Saddam had no WMD.

The same tension – if not straight contradiction – is found throughout the anti-war movement. Having said that it was absurd that Iraq was asked to prove a negative (it had no WMD), the fact that this same negative has been established is now used as a reason for questioning the rationale for the war. What was once impossible to prove is now assumed to be proven.

All this shows how confused people are about proving negatives. Often proving a negative is very easy indeed. If I say there is no wine left in my glass, a quick look verifies the fact. Contrary to received wisdom, absence of evidence can be evidence of absence. In law, there is also a presumption of innocence in the absence of evidence for guilt. It may not be possible to prove I didn't kill Colonel Mustard, but absence of evidence that I did is considered good enough evidence that I didn't.

The reason for accepting absence of evidence as positive evidence is precisely because proving a negative beyond all doubt is often impossible. So we have to be satisfied with something less than absolute proof. This something less is absence of evidence when evidence has been sought where it should be found.

The relationship between absence and evidence is therefore a complex one. At one extreme you have cases like the empty freezer, where the absence of evidence for the pizza being there proves that it isn't. At the other, you have an absence of evidence because no one has done a proper search for it, and that does not count as evidence of absence. In between, it's a question of judging how likely it is that something is the case, given the failure to turn up evidence for it. What absence of evidence means therefore varies according to circumstances.

There is no evidence that UFOs have landed in Nevada. There is no evidence that Ronald Reagan personally knew about the Iran/Contra scandal. The murderer left no evidence. There is no clear evidence that God exists. What are you entitled to conclude from these absences?

See also

55. Chance wouldn't be a fine thing

The no coincidence presumption

> A few weeks later, I was awakened by a phone call telling me I was going to be elected chief executive. I really don't believe it was a coincidence.
>
> Archie Dunham, *New York Times*[76]

Human beings have a tendency not to believe in coincidence. There are good, pragmatic reasons for this. Our ability to manipulate and predict the world depends on us being able to spot patterns of causation.

From an evolutionary point of view, it is better that we err on the side of seeing too many patterns than too few. For instance, say I plant some vegetables. I water them and talk to them, and they grow to be healthy. A person who sees more connections in nature than are really there would then both water and talk to the next batch, and would probably have a good crop. A person who is blind to associations might neither water nor talk to them and his crop would fail. As a rule of thumb, not assuming that events are merely coincidental gives us a greater chance of stumbling on relations which genuinely are connected.

In this way, nature is less interested in truth than in avoiding costly mistakes. If, however, we aspire to see things as they really are, we would do well to correct the natural impulse to presume a lack of coincidence.

Archie Dunham, chief executive of Conoco, provides a good example of how the no coincidence presumption can lead us to jump to unwarranted conclusions. Dunham recalls how in 1995, when he was executive vice president of Conoco, he was approached by headhunters who offered him a CEO position in another top company. Being a Christian, Dunham decided to pray, to help him decide whether to take the offer. 'Finally,' he recalls, 'I told God I was going to accept the position unless he stopped me. Two hours later the phone rang. It was the head of the search firm asking me to put my decision on hold because the board was talking to someone else. That was a clear signal for me to remain at Conoco.' A few weeks later, Dunham was elected chief executive of Conoco.

If you are a Christian, there is no reason to suppose that God might not intervene in this direct way. Nonetheless, why assume that is what actually happened? After all, in Dunham's case, it's not wildly improbable that a company set to hire him might have delayed for a while and that, being hot property, he got a promotion soon afterwards. In his position, with his beliefs, the rational thing would have been to suspend judgement. The evidence can't settle it. Yet his presumption is, as is so often the case, against accepting it was a coincidence. In a battle between two explanations, we usually choose the one which rules out the role of chance.

We seem to find it hard to accept that coincidences are bound to happen. It may seem amazing when I bump into an old friend I was thinking about only the day before, but, for every time that happens, I think of hundreds of people whom I don't fortuitously meet. What would be more amazing would be if I never met anyone I had recently been thinking about. In a random world, the complete absence of coincidences would need explaining, not their occurrence.

We also tend to overestimate just how much chance is needed for certain events to occur. A now well-known example of this is the question of how many people you need in a room before there is a 50–50 chance that two of them share a birthday. The answer is actually only twenty-three. Yet when people at a small gathering discover that two of them share a birthday, they tend think it is remarkably unlikely. Just because something seems remarkable doesn't mean that it is.

Test yourself: see how you react the next time you spot a coincidence. Are you too quick to assume there must be some real connection behind it? Or do you make the opposite mistake and fail to spot the tell-tale signs? (Partner wore best underwear the night they came home late?) And if you can't be perfect, which would you prefer: making too many connections or too few?

See also

56. It's your patriotic duty

Playing the loyalty card

Every patriotic American should heed the president's request.

House Speaker Dennis Hastert[77]

In 2000, the US House of Representatives was about to pass a resolution which would have described as 'genocide' the killing of 1.5 million Armenians in Turkey between 1915 and 1923. The Turkish government has always maintained that events in Armenia did not add up to genocide, claiming that there were deaths on both Turkish and Armenian sides of the conflict and that the killings were neither systematic nor centrally ordered. The subject is such a sensitive one in Turkey that charges were brought against the writer Orhan Pamuk simply for claiming that 'One million Armenians and 30,000 Kurds were killed in Turkey.'[78]

When the US House of Representatives looked set to recognize the genocide officially, Ankara responded forcefully. It threatened retaliation if the resolution was passed, which might have included grounding US military planes operating in Iraq from Turkish air bases and withdrawing from a $4.5 billion contract with a US military contractor.

These were certainly reasons to give House representatives pause for thought. But it was a pretty low move for House

Speaker Dennis Hastert to play the patriotism card as he pleaded for the resolution to be dropped.

For one thing, there are any number of reasons why a patriotic American could still have wanted to pass the resolution. She might have thought that Ankara's bark was worse than its bite. Turkey had made similar threats to France when its national assembly looked set to recognize the genocide earlier in the same year, but when it did so, nothing actually happened. You could also argue that to withdraw a resolution that says nothing false is to contravene the spirit of the First Amendment, which establishes Americans' freedom of expression. The US declared its independence to be free from the tyranny of foreign rule, so why was it now giving in to pressure from another sovereign state?

Playing the loyalty card also changes the rules of the game. Once you have said that something will be an act of disloyalty, you make it into one. Consider a domestic example. Your father doesn't talk to Uncle Fred, but you get on reasonably well with him, even though you think your father's grievances are justified. You don't believe talking to Fred is disloyal, because you think it is juvenile to suppose that one always has to side with one person completely in an argument. However, if your father tells you that he considers it an act of disloyalty to talk to Uncle Fred, his saying so in some sense makes it true. You have been forced to choose your loyalties where previously you could divide them.

In the case of patriotism it is more complicated because no one person, even the President, speaks for the whole nation. If your leader tells you that disagreeing with him is unpatriotic, the people can always decide to tell him it is no such thing. But if most of the nation rallies around the cause, dissenters do in some real sense become disloyal if they refuse to follow.

From a rational point of view, the main problem of appeals to loyalty – whether national, familial, tribal or any other kind – is that they bypass any serious discussion of the merits of a case. Instead of deciding what is true or false, we are forced to decide what is loyal or disloyal, when loyalty is not always the most important thing anyway. It was very disloyal of US army reservist Joe Darby to blow the whistle on what his comrades in arms were doing in Abu Ghraib prison, but it was right that he did so. Similarly, if you have ever had to face the agonizing choice between family loyalty and informing the police about ongoing violence by a close relative, I'd hope loyalty would go by the way, not justice.

Loyalty is rarely indivisible. Should a patriot be loyal to her government, her people, or to what she perceives as the interests or values of her country? Does loyalty to your family sometimes require disloyalty to individual members who tarnish its name? At work, is your primary loyalty to your team, department, office or company?

See also

57. Crack is my right

'It's a free country'

The directive would massively reduce the freedom of consumers to make their own informed choices.

Dr Robert Verkerk, executive director,
Alliance for Natural Health[79]

Wide generalizations are always dangerous, but I think it's fairly
safe to say that no politician ever stood for election on a platform
of reduced freedom for all. However, few of us are full-blown
libertarians who believe the state should do as close to nothing as
possible. Most of us actually want our governments to provide
health and education services, redistribute wealth to a lesser or
greater degree, and regulate many areas of public life.

Still, when laws come along that tamper with things we'd
personally prefer were left alone, it's a common ploy to insist that
the measures are wrong because 'it's a free country'. Such a claim
has strong rhetorical power, but it's actually pretty meaningless.

For example, in the UK and Ireland, smoking bans have
recently come into force which prohibit lighting up in all
enclosed public areas, including restaurants, cafés and bars. Many
complained that this was wrong because in a free country
people should be allowed to smoke if they wish. But most of
these people accept all sorts of other limits on freedom.

First, many judge that it would be easier and better for us if laws made some harmful activities much harder to perform. In one sense, it is true that someone is free to ruin their lives with crack cocaine if they so wish, but we would rather not be given the option, in order to protect ourselves and vulnerable others in moments of weakness. Anyone who agrees with this 'elective paternalism' has at least some reason for supporting limits on our freedom to smoke ourselves to death.

Second, our freedom is limited by the requirement not to harm others by its exercise. I may be free to smoke, but aren't others free to breathe clean air? Separate smoking areas are not a complete solution to this, because at the very least staff working in bars and restaurants have to go into them. You could argue that people don't have to work in smoky environments if they don't want to, but this may overestimate the extent to which those in often low-paid jobs have a meaningful choice as to where they work.

Dr Robert Verkerk's appeal to freedom was made in the context of an EU directive banning the sale of certain vitamin, herb and mineral supplements. Many of these are very popular, and Verkerk's organization, the Alliance for Natural Health, believes we should be free to buy them if we wish.

But again, the appeal to freedom is by itself empty. Almost everyone accepts the principle that people should not be allowed to sell anything and claim it is good for you. At best, this would lead to people selling modern-day 'snake oils' that do nothing at all; at worst, it would legitimate the selling of products that were actually dangerous. The EU directive was primarily about making sure that supplements were not sold unless they had been properly tested. In most other contexts, this would be not only uncontroversial but expected. Imagine the uproar if Coca-Cola added an untested ingredient to its drink which it claimed did you good. Why shouldn't supplements be treated in the same way?

Appealing to the freedom of consumers is a neat attention-grabbing ploy, but it cannot simply be asserted that we should be free to buy and sell just anything. Of course, the ANH does make the case for what it calls 'natural health products' (not very well, in my view), but when its spokespeople appeal to personal freedom, the argument is presented as though it needs no further justification. Saying 'it's a free country' is no substitute for a proper argument.

Do we have the right freedoms? Should we be free to end our own lives, if we so wish? Does our freedom to offend others extend to the right to enrage them provocatively? If I am free to say what I want, am I free to make untrue allegations about others in public? In a free country, isn't there a very long list of things I should not be free to do?

See also

58. Printed on 100 per cent fat-free paper!

Dubious advantages

> We want our people to be the best at hiring great man-
> agement . . . To do this well you need to get the kind of
> commitment you have in a first career, not a second one.
>
> Armstrong International advertisement[80]

The comic alter ego of Graham Fellows, the hapless singer-song-
writer John Shuttleworth, extolled the merits of a well-known
sports drink. 'It's isotonic,' he said, 'it cares for the environment.'

As with so much of the Shuttleworth act, behind the banal-
ity lies an astute observation. Like many of us, Shuttleworth is
easily impressed by the claims made by manufacturers and
advertisers for their products, even when he doesn't understand
what they mean. The mere fact that something is presented as
an advantage is enough to win him over.

In this case, Shuttleworth misunderstood what the alleged
advantages were. But on other occasions, if a claim is made
with sufficient strength, conviction or authority, it tends to be
accepted even if there is no real advantage at all. This trick
works best by presenting a claim which is factually correct but
irrelevant, in such a way as to make it appear like an advantage.

The classic version of this is used for foodstuffs which are
advertised as '95 per cent fat free' or similar. There is nothing

factually incorrect about this. But many will assume that it means the product is healthier, or is a better option if they are trying to lose weight. However, many such low-fat cakes, for example, are loaded with sugar and a serving can contain just as many calories as other regular-fat alternatives. The fact that something is 95 per cent fat free isn't necessarily an advantage at all, even though it is being sold to you as one.

Once you become alert to this, examples leap off the supermarket shelves and the advertising hoardings. Why is it good that something contains guarana if the amount it contains is less than that required for it to have any effect, assuming it does something desirable anyway? Why is it better that something comes in a new, bigger size, if the price has increased proportionally? Why should we rejoice that a cereal now comes in a foil bag when it was perfectly crispy in the old plastic one?

What makes the Armstrong International advertisement particularly interesting is that by spelling out so clearly why recruiting people starting their first career is supposed to be an advantage, they should have made its questionable nature clear. 'We do not generally employ people who have spent a career doing something else and who have turned to executive search as a second career,' they told us. Why on earth not? It just doesn't seem at all evident that people are more committed when on their first career than their second. Indeed, many people just drift into their first career, and the move to a second one often requires more commitment. And people on their second career have more experience of which kinds of people make great managers. Prima facie, then, the claim that this feature of their recruitment practices is an advantage is uncertain and it seems unlikely that any empirical evidence exists to back it up.

The presentation of dubious advantages probably works

because we are cognitive misers who like to make as few judgements as possible to get by. We prefer 'That's true' or 'That's false' to 'The factual part of that claim is true but its implied advantages are not real.' The latter requires us to distinguish the factual content from the evaluative implication of a claim, and when we're glancing at advertisements or product packaging that can be a cognitive task too many. It's not that we're stupid, it's just that we are already bombarded by commercial messages and we're doing all we can to filter them out.

There aren't many of us who are at our mentally sharpest when doing the shopping. Still, next time you go along a supermarket aisle, try to count the dubious advantages cited on packaging and posters. You might end with more examples on your list than you do groceries in your basket.

See also

59. Anyone would have done the same

'I was just doing my job'

Don't call me a hero. I was only doing my job.

Train driver Iain Black[81]

We often think 'I was only doing my job' is a bad argument because it is used to defend the indefensible. All sorts of brutality has been justified by this line, as though people had no choice in the matter. But you don't usually have to take a job that requires you to be nasty, and even once employed, there is often a choice between rigidly following procedures and showing some flexibility. You don't always have to cut off an old person's electricity supply, take children from their parents or fine someone for an innocent mistake.

But bad arguments are not used only for ignoble aims or to back up false claims. There are times when we employ faulty arguments for entirely honourable purposes. This was true of Iain Black, the driver of a London to Glasgow train which derailed on 23 February 2007 in Cumbria.

The crash was caused by a points failure, which the driver could do nothing about. One person died and twenty-two others were injured, a toll which could have been higher had Black not stayed at the controls of the train on full-brake for half a mile as it came off the tracks. He spent three and a half weeks in hospital and, at the time of writing, had still not totally recovered.

No wonder he was hailed as a hero. But Black denied the accolade, saying, 'I just did what any train driver would have done and it was very much an automatic thing.'

Firefighters, soldiers, police officers and rescue workers frequently dismiss claims that they have acted heroically. To some extent, they are often right. In the aftermath of disasters, society needs to identify its heroes, to find something elevating in the human spirit to counteract the deflation of disaster. People simply doing what they were trained to do are portrayed as though they were acting exceptionally.

However, often people really do act in extraordinary ways. They don't just do their jobs, they go over and above the call of duty. To claim they do not is no less an untruth for being motivated by commendable humility.

Iain Black used a second fallacious argument, when he said he just acted automatically. The assumption underlying this is that if we do not deliberate before we act, we deserve no credit for it. This is a highly questionable premise. As Aristotle argued, being good is largely a matter of cultivating certain habits. The generous person need not always think carefully before offering something to someone, because she may simply have nurtured traits in her character that dispose her towards generosity. Bravery is just the same: a person who has cultivated the virtues of bravery will be able to act courageously without having to build up courage first.

Sport provides good examples of how real merit can go hand in hand with thoughtless action. The best football players have such well-developed skills that they often pull off brilliant moves without even thinking. People talk about 'split-second decisions' but it is usually more accurate to say there is no conscious decision at all. Players who can do this are rightly considered better than those who can perform the same moves only after careful pre-planning.

Nor do we regard the automatic nature of an action as an excuse for wrongdoing. If someone says that they should be forgiven for punching someone because it was automatic, or they drove away after running over a child for the same reason, we would consider that a lousy defence. If we are willing to blame people for their automatic actions, we should be willing to offer praise for them too.

The case of Iain Black reflects the wider point that sometimes bad arguments are entirely benign. Philosophy and critical thinking teach you to see the flaws in someone's reasoning. What they don't always do is tell you how much they really matter.

How often do you, or people close to you, hide behind roles or identities when justifying what you say or do? Is it true that 'any parent would do the same'? Are you too quick to do things you don't like or disapprove of because you think they are part and parcel of your work? Do you sometimes act like you think a Christian, Muslim, atheist, socialist or conservative should, without stopping to ask if this is really required of you?

See also

60. Someone must pay

Zero sums that don't add up

For every winner, there have to be corresponding losers, and it has nothing to do with skill, 'investing' or how popular you are.

Neil Collins, *Daily Telegraph*[82]

Like many opponents of the 'something-for-nothing culture', Neil Collins seems to believe not only that it is true but a moral imperative, that someone, somewhere has to pay for everything good which is done. Collins wrote about the 'baby bonds' scheme where the British government pays a lump sum into an investment fund for every child when it is born. Governments may decide to add to it at future birthdays and relatives may also contribute up to £1,000 per year. Babies from poor families receive more from the government than their better-off peers. The thinking behind the scheme is that a little capital at the start of adult life can make a big difference between success and failure.

Sceptics have found much to doubt in the scheme, not least the paltry sums involved – no more than £500 initially from the government, which is hardly going to force open many doors for an eighteen-year-old. But what seems to irritate Collins most is his conviction that, even if it makes some people better off, someone will have to pay for all this. That means on balance it's no help at all – what the government dishes out with one hand it will have to take back with another.

But is it true that for every winner there has to be a corresponding loser? Whichever way you interpret this supposed piece of common sense, it doesn't seem so.

Could it mean that the total amount of wealth in a society must always remain the same, so any increase in one person's wealth must lead to a decrease in someone else's? Evidently not, since the world has got richer. It's easy to see how: finding more resources or using them more productively increases wealth. So a primitive society that produced only food and bricks (and whose wealth could be measured only in these commodities) would be richer if it learned how to grow food and make bricks more productively. Bigger houses, more food, and no losers.

Could it mean that any increase in government spending has to be matched by an increase in taxation or a cut elsewhere? Not necessarily. All that is needed to fuel higher government spending is a higher tax yield. If the economy grows faster than inflation, tax rates can remain the same and government spending can increase in real terms, since there is a bigger fiscal pie for the government to take a proportionately identical slice out of. This is why, counterintuitively, sometimes decreasing tax rates can lead to an increase in the overall tax yield.

Could it mean, more vaguely, that if someone benefits, someone else must pay in some way, even if these benefits and payments are not strictly financial? Again, there's no reason to think so. There may be ways, for example, to help convicted criminals reassimilate into society, and since criminals cost the taxpayer whereas working people contribute to national wealth, such a scheme would benefit criminals, taxpayers and society alike.

The principle that for every winner there has to be a corresponding loser just doesn't hold: there are such things as win–win situations. The difficulty comes when we have to distinguish them from zero-sum games, like tennis, where there can be only one winner.

Does the internet provide a forum in which everyone can get their music or thoughts out there, or is it still the case that, as in the physical world, finite time and resources mean there can be only a few winners? Is carbon offsetting for flights a win-win or a green-washing con? Does fairtrade coffee mean 'great coffee for you and a great deal for producers' or is there someone, somewhere, paying for it all?

See also

61. Lies, damned lies and statistics

The abuse and misuse of numbers

A few years ago the NSPCC asked thousands of people whether they had been sexually abused involving physical contact before they were twelve years old. Sixteen per cent of women and 7 per cent of men said they had. This equates to one in nine pre-teenage children. The conclusion is that 1 million children are being abused in Britain right now.

Mark Easton, BBC homes affairs correspondent[83]

Accurate statistics are just facts, and as such, they don't lie. Nevertheless, the bad reputation they have as being the source of the darkest deceptions is not entirely unfounded. For the very indisputability of a statistic can transfix us, leaving us blind to the unproven fact it is supposed to demonstrate.

Mark Easton's pithy run through some statistics surrounding child abuse is a masterclass in how not to use numbers. His conclusion, on one of the nation's top news broadcasts, is truly shocking: '1 million children are being abused in Britain right now'. You would hope that a top BBC journalist would make sure this statement was backed up by facts. If only.

With any statistical data, the first question has to be: what is its source? Where do these numbers come from? To his credit, Easton does tell us. They come from a survey by the NSPCC –

the National Society for the Prevention of Cruelty to Children. This in itself should make us cautious: an organization whose *raison d'être* is to protect us from something has a vested interest in making us feel that we need it. Some scepticism would therefore be advised.

The next question should be, what was the methodology? The NSPCC asked adults whether they had been abused as children. Is this an accurate way of knowing whether such abuse took place? Probably not. But even if it is, there is still a clear problem: the survey can tell us only about past abuse. What is going on right now may be quite different. In the UK, charities like the NSPCC and Childline have been successful in highlighting the prevalence of abuse and encouraging children to report it. It would not be surprising if, as a result, incidence of abuse has decreased.

So we have various reasons for treating the statistics with caution. But then Easton delivers the conclusion: '1 million children are being abused in Britain right now'. This just is not what the survey shows. In addition to the problem of inferring present activity from a survey of past events, the study did not show that at any one time 16 per cent of women and 7 per cent of men were being physically abused. Rather, these statistics refer to abuse at any time during childhood. It is irresponsible sensationalism to claim that the study suggests such terrible levels of abuse are going on at the present moment.

Hence Easton's short summary contains at least three common mistakes when reporting statistics: failure to provide caveats as to the source of the numbers; applying facts gathered in one context to a different one; and simplistically drawing unwarranted conclusions on the basis of the numbers.

There are numerous other ways of abusing statistics. For

instance, a report in the *Guardian* a few years ago claimed that the publishing industry 'lacks cultural diversity' because 'only' 13 per cent of people who work in it belong to minority ethnic groups.[84] What the report did not mention, however, was that at the time, ethnic minorities made up only around 8 per cent of the UK population. As often happens, the statistics were presented as though they speak for themselves, when comparators and interpretations are essential.

Do the following statistics speak for themselves? Working women with children are significantly happier than stay-at-home mothers, regardless of how many hours they work.[85] Nearly a third of Scots think there is sometimes good reason to be prejudiced against minority groups.[86] People wait an average of seventeen minutes to get technical help from their broadband provider.[87] Children in England feel less safe at school than those in comparable countries.[88] Do you really understand the significance of these findings or do you find yourself assuming you do without sufficient cause? Do these statistics lie, or is it just that we don't read them carefully enough?

See also

62. Who says smoking kills?

You can't prove it

Cigarette smoking has not been scientifically established as a cause of lung cancer. The cause or causes of lung cancer are unknown.

Imperial Tobacco legal documents[89]

'Prove it' looks like a fair challenge to issue to anyone making a claim you suspect to be false. And properly understood, that's just what it is. The problem is that an adequate 'proof' almost always leaves a space for the shadow of unreasonable doubt.

The quest for certainty goes back at least as far as Plato. In *The Republic*, Plato made it clear that the highest form of knowledge is of certain, immutable truths. Absolute certainty has been the goal of many philosophers ever since.

However, hardly anyone now thinks that absolute certainty is possible in most spheres of human knowledge. David Hume's distinction between matters of fact and relations of ideas is useful here. The latter include mathematics, logic and statements which are true by definition. The former include all truths about the actual world. Hume pointed out that we cannot establish these truths according to the strict methods of deduction which we use with, say, mathematics. Rather, past experience provides evidence for their truth, evidence which is never logically watertight, but which we can judge to be sufficient.

Take as a simple example the boiling point of water. Logically, it does not follow from the fact that all water to date has boiled at 100° Celsius (adjusting for impurities and air pressure, of course) that all future water will do the same. But that doesn't matter, because facts about the world aren't established by strict logical deduction. Rather, they are determined by a process of generalization from past experience. As Stephen Jay Gould put it, 'In science, "fact" can only mean "confirmed to such a degree that it would be perverse to withhold provisional assent". I suppose that apples might start to rise tomorrow, but the possibility does not merit equal time in physics classrooms.'[90]

It should be obvious that no facts about the world can ever be proved beyond all doubt whatsoever. Matters become murkier, however, when we get to facts for which there is overwhelming evidence, but not quite as much as for our most well-established truths. Here is where we come across cases such as smoking's relation to cancer. Although there is very strong evidence that smoking is a major cause of lung cancer, there is wiggle-room available for the sceptic to demand a higher standard of proof and claim that science has not yet met it. Not all alternative explanations have been ruled out and it remains at least possible that smoking is not a major causal factor at all.

We should not be fooled by such sophistry. The fact that other explanations are logically possible is a red herring. The fact that it is possible science has got it wrong is also uninteresting: science is by its nature fallible and to demand infallibility from it is to disobey Aristotle's wise injunction to expect only as much precision as the subject matter allows. Like the connoisseur of good vodka, the truth seeker should not demand 100 per cent proof. We have to live with a small measure of uncertainty. Proof requires us to move only beyond reasonable doubt. It cannot require us to remove all possibility of doubt whatsoever.

There is a twist to this tale, however. Although a lack of certain proof should not make us suspend judgement, it is worth remembering that even our most widely accepted scientific facts may turn out to be wrong. The philosopher of science Hasok Change, for instance, has written about how the boiling point of water depends not only on purity and air pressure but what sort of container it is boiled in.[91] Apparently many engineers know this full well, but most people are still convinced the science has shown water boils at 100° C. So while we should not allow the element of doubt to leave us suspending judgement, it should make us remember to leave the door open to evidence that might shake up even our most confidently held beliefs. Walking the tightrope between excessive scepticism and its proportionate cousin, however, is not an easy thing to do.

Playing at scepticism is a good way of realizing that lack of absolute certainty is the rule rather than the exception. Try taking virtually any belief you hold with some conviction and ask yourself why you might not be justified in holding it to be certainly true. Think of reasons why it might actually be false. This exercise can be disturbing, but it should help you take a balanced approach to degrees of uncertainty.

See also

63. Counsellors stole my friends

Cui bono?

> Our friends have been stolen from us by those who seek to make a fast buck from their absence.

Carol Sarler, The Times[92]

Like many people, I've got dozens of friends. Facebook friends, that is: a rag-bag assortment of virtual buddies including people I once knew but haven't seen for years, professional colleagues and total strangers. However, when it comes to real friends, people we see regularly, confide in, and just enjoy passing time with, we are becoming worse off. A study in the *American Sociological Review* showed that over the past twenty years, the average circle of close friends has shrunk by a third.

Pondering the causes of this in *The Times*, Carol Sarler reached a rather startling conclusion: she blamed 'the monstrously expanding counselling trade' for encouraging us to talk to shrinks rather than our friends.

She reached this 'inescapable conclusion' by asking a simple question: *cui bono?* Who benefits? The logic of this is that since it is to the advantage of counsellors that we have fewer friends, it is rational to conclude that the rise of counselling is to blame for the fact that we have so few.

I know journalists are paid to have outrageous opinions, but this is surely going beyond the call of duty. But Sarler is not alone in placing great faith in the ability of the *cui bono*? question to unlock the secret causes of all sorts of beliefs and practices.

For instance, AA Gill thinks it is 'helpful' to ask who benefits from climate change scepticism. His answer is 'Obviously, people who drill oil wells, own power stations or appear on popular motoring programmes all have an interest in global warming being none of our business.'[93] But the question could just as easily be turned around: who benefits from the belief that man-made global warming is a real and present danger? Luddites, environmentalists, pessimists, alternative energy businesses and the owners of the *Independent* newspaper, which fills a large number of its pages with grim tales of how we're going to hell in a handcart. Every point of view benefits someone, but nonetheless some happen to be true.

The belief that *cui bono*? is a question that leads directly to the truth is particularly evident in many far-left analyses of US foreign policy. The claim that US (and often UN) actions are performed solely to benefit American capitalists (rather than the American people) has become such a commonplace that many believe it can simply be assumed that this is always the case. The function of *cui bono*? then becomes to explain all world events in terms of the benefit to the US. So, if things go badly in Iraq, that is because it benefits American capitalists to fight an expensive, protracted war. If things go well, it is because it benefits American capitalists to have a peaceful 'client state' for its contractors to go into and clean up. Events lose any explanatory power because the question of who benefits already has a predetermined answer.

The tragedy of all this is that *cui bono*? is actually a very good question to ask, and often it does point you towards the truth. For instance, the British press recently reported on a 'study' which showed that eating chocolate gave you more pleasure than kissing. Who would benefit from this factoid? Chocolate manufacturers, of course. And who was behind the study? You've got it. But it is critical to realize even here that unless and until we know that those with an interest in an outcome engineered it, *cui bono*? does no more than raise our suspicion. *Cui bono*? is a good question, not a skeleton key to the truth.

What other suspicions raised by the *cui bono*? question point to the truth and which are false alarms? The belief that condoms help prevent the spread of STDs benefits condom manufacturers? The fact that the desire to travel benefits airlines? The truth that anxiety about body image benefits the beauty industry? Do these facts tell us anything we should be worried about?

See also

64. No one made you do it

Choice makes everything all right

In a typical developing nation, if you're able to work for an American multinational, you make eight times the average wage. That's why people are lining up to get these jobs.

Johan Norberg, *In Defence of Global Capitalism*[94]

Do you ever worry about all the exploited people in the world? Perhaps you worry too much. Sure, draw the line at slaves, but when it comes to the likes of sex workers, people who work in sweatshops, soldiers who get shot, or the people who have to clean the toilets you use, you can always tell yourself: they didn't have to do it – it was their choice.

The key concept here is 'informed consent'. If someone is tricked into prostitution, or told they are going to be paid well and actually given a pittance, that's one thing. But if they take on a job in the full knowledge of what they are getting into, no matter how dangerous or unpleasant it is, shouldn't we just assume they are making a rational choice for themselves and not agonize over their plight?

It's a reassuring argument since, if it works, our consciences can be cleared. But the idea that there is no problem as long as there is consent is flawed for several reasons.

First, people sometimes have to choose terrible things because in practical terms they have no choice. Prostitution is a good example. I'm sure there are some women for whom sex work is not a last resort but a deliberate career move, but in many cases they are driven to it out of desperation. Any man who thinks prostitution is never exploitative as long as the woman isn't being physically forced into it is surely deluded.

Second, the fact that something unpleasant is the best choice available to someone doesn't make it OK, if they could be offered something better at little or no cost. For example, managers in factories in the developing world often refuse their workers sufficient toilet breaks, deny them drinking water, and fail to follow local laws or health and safety procedures – the list could go on. So what if working in one of these places is still the best option locally? If Western consumers paying a little bit more could remove all these hardships, why not do it?

Johan Norberg makes many pertinent points about the benefits of trade with developing countries, but he makes too much of the fact that jobs for American multinationals are often the most sought-after. People may be queuing up to take them, but people queue up for all sorts of things when they're in dire need. He also throws in a red herring when he says, 'If workers were paid US wages in Vietnam, employers wouldn't be able to hire them.' The choice is not between sweatshops or Western pay and conditions, it's between the opportunity to earn a decent living in a decent job or working long hours in poor conditions for barely enough to live on.

The issue of informed consent is also relevant in contexts in which people are asked to sign away their legal rights on the basis that they have been told the risks and benefits and agree to them. This happens a lot in medicine, where people need to agree to taking drugs or having operations. But how free are we really to withhold our consent? Your doctor knows more than you, so don't you just have to trust her judgement? If it proves badly wrong, it's not enough for the hospital simply to say you gave your permission so you shouldn't complain.

For it truly to be the case that making a choice means it is no one else's business what happens to you, the choice has to be genuinely informed, a real rather than a forced one, and what people do to you subsequently still has to be as fair as can be reasonably expected of them.

Can we honestly say these conditions for informed, free consent are met for sex workers, people who work in sweatshops, soldiers who get shot or the people who have to clean the toilets you use? If not, what are those not directly responsible for the exploitation to do about it? Do you have a responsibility to make sure what you buy has not been made by people working in unjust conditions?

See also

4. 'If I don't, somebody else will'
17. Won't and shouldn't
51. Legality and morality
59. 'I was just doing my job'

65. If it weren't for you, they'd still be alive

Cause is not responsibility

The brutal violations practised by the American and British occupying forces against Iraqi prisoners at Abu Ghraib prison led to retaliating responses against Americans in Iraq. The pictures of rape and torture . . . forced Abu Musab al-Zarqawi's group to execute an American citizen by the sword.

Egyptian newspaper *Al-Wafd*[95]

On 7 May 2004, the American civilian Nick Berg was brutally decapitated by members of the Islamist group Muntada al-Ansar in Iraq. We know this because the group videoed the whole appalling process and posted the film online.

The question of who was responsible for this death was, in one sense, easily answered: Muntada al-Ansar. However, the group themselves laid the blame squarely at the feet of the US government, claiming that mistreatment of prisoners at Abu Ghraib prison was the real cause of Berg's slaughter. 'We tell you that the dignity of the Muslim men and women in Abu Ghraib and others is not redeemed except by blood and souls. You will not receive anything from us but coffins after coffins,' they said in their statement.

Many seemed prepared to buy this line. The Egyptian

newspaper *Al-Wafd* went so far as to say that Abu Ghraib 'forced' the group to execute Berg. (It is chilling how the phrase 'by the sword' possesses a kind of nobility that Berg's murder did not: his head was sawn off slowly with a knife.)

It is not unusual for responsibility to be assigned using this kind of rationale. After 9/11 many people said or insinuated that 'America had it coming' because of its actions in the Middle East.

Behind these arguments are simple factual claims. 9/11 would not have happened if American foreign policy had been different; Nick Berg would not have been executed if Abu Ghraib had not happened. Therefore, the American government has to shoulder at least some of the responsibility for the attacks on the Twin Towers and the execution of one of its citizens.

Here we have to be very careful, because there are at least two different senses in which someone or something can be 'responsible' or 'to blame'. One is morally neutral: a loose bolt can be 'responsible' or 'to blame' for a car crash but that does not mean it should be sued. 'Responsible' in this sense merely means something is a critical causal factor. Likewise, a woman who walks alone at night in a quite dangerous area and is raped is only 'responsible' for this in the very limited sense that her recklessness was a causal factor. She did not 'have it coming' and any moral blame lies squarely with the rapist.

So even if we accept that American actions in the Middle East were at least partially causally responsible for Nick Berg's murder and the 9/11 attacks, it does not necessarily follow that America is morally to blame for what happened. The identification of a critical causal factor does not automatically lead to a placing of responsibility. For instance, Nick Berg's father told

CBS news that his son, a Jew, had a fringed religious cloth with him, and that 'If there was any doubt that they were going to kill him that probably clinched it, I'm guessing.'[96] The conclusion here is that it is possible that if Nick Berg had not been Jewish, he would not have been executed. If that were the case, does that mean that his Jewishness is morally to blame for his death? The suggestion is absurd. Moral responsibility does not just follow any old cause.

To be responsible for something in the moral sense, it must be the case that one actually did the terrible deed, created a situation where causing harm was a morally justified response, or behaved recklessly in the knowledge of what terrible consequences might follow.

Were the destruction of the Twin Towers and the murder of Nick Berg justified responses to US foreign policy? If not (as surely we must answer), did US foreign policy create conditions in which such unjustified responses were nonetheless made very probable? If so, how much moral responsibility can be pinned on the government?

See also

66. Prove yourself

False authorities

> After reading *Captive State*, I will never be able to take the Labour government seriously again.
>
> Thom Yorke, lead singer of Radiohead[97]

In my opinion – which has never been humble – Radiohead are the best rock band on the planet right now. Along with Goldfrapp, they are one of only two groups whose latest album I would buy (or download for free) as soon as it comes out, without listening to it or reading reviews first.

But although I am prepared to acknowledge the genius of Thom Yorke & Co. in the realm of music, and I know Yorke warbled 'Don't question my authority' on the song '2 + 2 = 5', that's just what we should do. Why should his endorsement of a purportedly serious book on 'the corporate takeover of Britain' be considered worth splashing over the dust jacket? Why should we value his opinion on this more than we do that of my aunt Mabel? Yorke is not an authority in matters of politics and the only reason what he says on the subject is taken seriously is that he is very popular for reasons totally unconnected with current affairs. Celebrities get to mouth off about whatever they want and people listen.

This is just an extreme example of how people are often treated as 'authorities' on certain subjects for no good reason. If all false authorities were so obvious there would be little point in drawing attention to them. But they're not. For instance, the science writer Ben Goldacre has done as thorough a job as could be imagined showing that we should not take the so-called 'nutritional expert' Gillian McKeith to be a reliable authority. Until a case was taken to the Advertising Standards Authority about her, she used to go by the title 'Dr' despite the fact that her PhD was gained by correspondence course from a non-accredited American college. Goldacre has shown how many of her pronouncements on nutrition make elementary mistakes about biology, yet some Scottish Conservatives have called for her to advise the government, and in 2005 the Soil Association gave her a Consumer Education Award.

The phenomenon of people being granted the questionable status of an authority is most problematic in the sphere of morality. In medical ethics, the opinions of doctors are often given great weight. The *Daily Telegraph*, for example, ran a story about a leading transplant surgeon, Professor Nadey Hakim, who called for the legalization of trade in human organs. But why should a surgeon be in a better position to pronounce on the ethics of organ sales than, say, Thom Yorke? Hakim's expertise is in surgery, not ethics.

This is a tricky area, for arguably there is no such thing as an expert in ethics – at least there are no experts to whom we should all defer in the same way as there are experts in engineering or medicine. But there are people better qualified than others to examine and deal with complex moral issues. The media tend to focus on what doctors, bishops, leaders of pressure groups and pundits have to say. We tend to hear less from members of ethics commissions and moral philosophers, who think about these problems in much more depth than anyone else but do not get the chance to contribute as much to the debates as they deserve.

The problem of false authorities is thus much more widespread and sometimes much less obvious than it is in the extreme case of the singer–cum–political commentator.

Once you do start to question why some people's opinions are given automatic respect, you soon find yourself realizing how few genuine authorities there are. Next time you listen to a radio news programme, for example, take note of who they invite on to give 'expert analysis and commentary'. You'll find that often they aren't authorities on the subject being discussed at all. I should know: sometimes it's me.

See also

31.   Arguments from authority
50.   Vacuous pseudo-wisdom
88.   Fallacy of ancient wisdom
94.   'It's not for you to say'

67. Kris Kristofferson is a lizard

'I'm entitled to my opinion'

My own view is that the Prince has a perfect right to speak about subjects that interest him.

Boris Johnson, London mayoral candidate[98]

In the 1980s, David Icke was one of Britain's most famous sports broadcasters. Then he had a series of 'spiritual' experiences, and in an interview on the country's top-rated chat show, *Wogan*, announced that he was the son of God and that Britain would soon be devastated by tidal waves and earthquakes. He instantly became a figure of ridicule. But he bounced back, and has now published several books and given numerous talks outlining his idiosyncratic worldview. His most notorious belief is that the world is ruled by a secret group of reptilian humanoids called the Illuminati, who count among their number George W. Bush, Queen Elizabeth II and Kris Kristofferson.

Icke is certainly 'entitled to his opinion'. But what does that actually mean in practice? For instance, after Icke started talking about his unorthodox view, the Green Party, for whom he was a spokesperson, stopped him speaking publicly on their behalf. Was Icke being gagged? If he was entitled to his opinion, wasn't he also entitled to give it? After all, there can be no genuine freedom of belief in a country where you are obliged to keep any dissenting opinions to yourself.

However, too often we play the 'I'm entitled to my opinion' card as though it trumps all other considerations, when in reality it obviously does not.

First, there are cases where the expression of an opinion is likely to have concrete, detrimental consequences. Telling an angry mob that you think (incorrectly) that their ire should be directed at the local Hindus could lead to harm coming to the innocent. Expressing other racist or sexist views can also influence people's decisions to employ people of a particular ethnic origin or gender, such as when it is claimed that certain social groups are lazier or less intelligent than others. It's no use saying one is entitled to one's opinion in such situations: words can cause things to happen, and they must be used carefully.

Second, the fact that you have a right to your views does not mean that you should be provided with somewhere prominent to voice them. This point was missed by many in the UK when a controversy arose about the Oxford Union's decision to host a debate with the leader of the far-right British National Party Nick Griffin, and the revisionist historian David Irving. Many people thought the Union's decision was a disgrace, provoking the predictable response that no one should be gagged in a free society. This misses the point: no one was trying to gag Griffin or Irving. As the *Economist* put it succinctly in a leader comment: 'They are entitled to their opinions, but not to a privileged platform for them at Oxford.'[99]

Prince Charles, so stoutly defended by the comedic Conservative politician Boris Johnson, has often spoken out on controversial matters, calling for more alternative medicine, such as homeopathy; saying that McDonald's should be banned; and making pleas for traditional instead of modernist architecture. He is entitled to his opinion but, as unelected heir to the throne, his views receive greater attention than those of others. He has no power but, purely because of an accident of birth, he does have influence.

In the United Kingdom's constitutional monarchy, the royal family are not supposed to interfere with the political process except *in extremis*. Is it not the case, therefore, that when Charles offers opinions on matters which are the subject of public policy, he sometimes oversteps his constitutional role and abuses his privileged position? If so, his right to his opinions does not entail an unfettered right to use any opportunity he has to promulgate them.

In a free society, allowing diversity of opinion is not a straightforward matter but a highly complex one.

Although it is true that no one is obliged to give people a platform for unorthodox views, if no such platforms were ever given we would end up with stifling conformity. The question therefore becomes where and when is it appropriate for maverick, offensive opinions to be aired? How does the mass media avoid both giving undue credence to cranks and becoming a mere defender of received opinion?

See also

68. God don't ride no reindeer

Missing the point

> Dawkins often compares belief in God to an infantile belief in Santa Claus or the Tooth Fairy, saying it is something we should all outgrow. But the analogy is flawed. How many people do you know who started to believe in Santa Claus in adulthood?
>
> Alister McGrath, theologian[100]

Richard Dawkins is not exactly the most diplomatic of atheism's ambassadors. Nor is he particularly kind to his opponents. Several books have been written as direct responses to his best-selling *The God Delusion*, but he refers to their authors as 'fleas', inspired by Yeats's line 'Was there ever a dog that praised its fleas?'

One such 'flea' is Alister McGrath, whose book *The Dawkins Delusion?* was published only four months after the book it dissected. McGrath is no intellectual slouch, but even he seems to have fallen prey to a common error when criticizing Dawkins, which is to miss completely the point of some of his arguments.

Dawkins is not the first person to compare belief in God with belief in mythical beings such as Father Christmas, the Tooth Fairy or the Flying Spaghetti Monster. Using this analogy is typical of the weakness of Dawkins as a rhetorician, since while the comparison tends to delight atheists, believers and those sympathetic to belief tend to find it dismissive and offensive. However, McGrath's response is more indicative of his own logical failings than of Dawkins's.

Whenever an analogy is used in an argument, it is important to see what part of the comparison is pertinent. For example, when Robert Burns wrote 'My love is like a red red rose' he did not mean that it grows in soil, needs watering and looks nice cut in a vase. Likewise, to say that belief in God is like belief in Santa Claus does not mean that it is confined to early childhood and entails that God has a reindeer called Rudolph. The point of the analogy for Dawkins is the evidential basis for belief. God is like Santa Claus and the Tooth Fairy, says Dawkins, in that some people believe in him, but there is no evidence that he exists. He deliberately uses an example of something we know does not exist, because he wants to make the point that the evidential case for God is no stronger than it is for these childhood fantasies.

That argument can be challenged: perhaps you think there is evidence for the existence of the Judaeo-Christian God. But the argument is simply not addressed if an irrelevant aspect of the analogy is taken to be significant instead. This is what McGrath does. He says the analogy doesn't work because people start believing in God as adults, whereas they adopt belief in Santa only as kids. This is irrelevant. Dawkins's point had nothing to do with the age at which people adopt beliefs; it was all about evidence.

In my experience, people often miss the point of analogies. They tend to assume that you're drawing all sorts of parallels when in fact you're just trying to draw out one. But there are plenty of other ways of missing the point (a fallacy formally

212

known as *ignoratio elenchi*). For instance, in debates over abortion, 'pro-choice' campaigners often respond to arguments about the status of the foetus as a human being by appealing to the rights of the mother. Whatever the merits of the maternal rights case, if the argument against abortion is that it is tantamount to murder, you can't respond to it unless you take on that claim. Talk of the mother's rights is often just changing the subject, and so missing the point.

It's easy to miss the point because we tend to get used to seeing issues that concern us from a very particular perspective. It takes some intellectual imagination to be able to see differently. For instance, when we describe a killing as 'senseless' are we often just failing to see what sense it has for the killers? If someone defends drug legalization solely for reasons of personal liberty, isn't it missing the point to respond by claiming that such a move would lead to more deaths? Isn't missing the point so easy because we tend to assume too readily that we know what the point is?

See also

69. Sparring with scarecrows

The straw man fallacy

> Free-market capitalism is founded on one value: the max-
> imization of profit. Other values, like human dignity and
> solidarity, or environmental sustainability, are disregarded
> as soon as they limit potential profit.
>
> Naomi Klein, *No Logo*[101]

Nasty, greedy folk, these free market capitalists. If, as I suspect, you hold values other than the maximization of profit, you can't possibly be on their side. Better to join the anti-capitalists, for whom human dignity, solidarity and environmental sustainability count for something.

If Klein's moral victory over capitalism seems too easy, that's because it is. The problem becomes evident when you ask yourself what this demonic free-market capitalism actually is.

It certainly isn't the free market of economic theory, which is in itself value-neutral. Everything depends on how the economic actors behave within that market. People could base their purchasing decisions entirely on price. But equally, they could base them on environmental or human impact. Nothing about free-market capitalism would compel people to cast off all values other than profit. The growth in sales of fairtrade coffee, for example, is driven by demand in the market from values-conscious consumers.

Nor is Klein's capitalism the one instantiated in Western liberal democracies. There, all sorts of mechanisms exist to limit potential profits in the name of other values, most obviously: competition laws, minimum wages, health and safety regulations, taxes and environmental legislation. If actually existing capitalism is the target, Klein has missed by a mile.

So what was her target? Her comments were in a response to the question of how consumers can make ethical purchasing decisions. It is thus clearly about actually existing capitalism, not how it might be. And as we have seen, the idea that profit trumps all else in this world doesn't stand up to the slightest scrutiny.

Klein's argument is an example of the straw man fallacy. Although her target is the actual, essentially capitalist, economic system of Western liberal democracies, she has not in fact confronted its reality. Instead, she has set up as a target a caricature and attacked that instead. But her subsequent easy victory over it is seen as a victory over the real McCoy.

Put in general terms, the straw man fallacy occurs when you deal with a weaker or distorted version of an argument or position as though it were in fact the full and accurate one. The position itself is then taken to be flawed even though it has not actually been subject to proper critique at all.

Although the misrepresentations characteristic of straw men can be wilful, often they simply reflect how little effort we make to understand our opponents' points of view. Why should we? If we attribute hopelessly inadequate or repugnant views to others, the virtues of our own commitments seem obvious. But if we grant that our enemies have an arguable case, then our own views suddenly do not seem so unassailable, and our opponents not so clearly on the side of the devil.

Another explanation for the popularity of straw men is that if we win an argument, we feel that our opinions have been vindicated, even if our victory was won over an emaciated opponent. We forget that the aim of rational debate is not for *us* to win, but for the *truth* to win. That is rarely what happens when the fight is with a straw man.

Sometimes it is hard to see which party in the debate is jousting with a straw man, or whether the whole debate is being fought by scarecrows. For instance, Richard Dawkins is often accused of attacking a straw man version of religion, characterized by irrational, literal belief in myths. But Dawkins is frequently reduced to a straw man by his enemies too. Mary Midgley once famously criticized his selfish gene hypothesis by saying that 'genes cannot be selfish or unselfish, any more than atoms can be jealous, elephants abstract or biscuits teleological.'[102] But Dawkins agrees that genes have no motives: this is not how he meant the phrase 'selfish gene' at all. So who are the real straw men in the Dawkins debates?

See also

70. Nothing but the truth

Half truths

I did not have sexual relations with that woman, Miss Lewinsky.

Bill Clinton[103]

Imagine a seventeen-year-old boy from a conservative family who has experience of oral sex, mutual masturbation and so on, but not penetrative sex. 'Are you a virgin?' ask his parents. 'Yes,' the boy replies. 'Are you a virgin?' ask his friends. 'Dur, no!' comes the reply. One of these answers must be true, but it turns out that both are misleading.

When Clinton looked straight into the camera and said he had not had sexual relations with Monica Lewinsky, he was talking as the boy was to his parents. He chose to interpret 'sexual relations' as being a euphemism for full sexual intercourse in a context where most people listening to him wanted to know about intimate sexual behaviour more generally. He was playing on the ambiguity of the term to state a half-truth: a statement which can be read as being literally true, but which occludes other important relevant truths.

Half or partial truths in themselves are not only perfectly acceptable, they are absolutely necessary. To tell the whole truth about any event would be too massive a burden. Telling a truthful story requires knowing what to leave out as well as what to leave in. Problems come only when the suppression of certain details makes what one says misleading. Lawyers have the useful phrase *suggestio falsi* for this: when you say something that is factually correct, but which suggests a falsehood. An all too familiar example is the husband who declares that he was not with another woman last night, knowing full well he was with her the night before.

In the Clinton case, the half-truth was seen through pretty quickly. But what about this statement from Tony Blair to the British parliament on 24 September 2002?

> It [the UK intelligence dossier] concludes that Iraq has chemical and biological weapons, that Saddam has continued to produce them, that he has existing and active military plans for the use of chemical and biological weapons, which could be activated within forty-five minutes, including against his own Shia population; and that he is actively trying to acquire nuclear weapons capability.

The British government and Tony Blair vigorously defended the notorious forty-five minute claim as an accurate statement about what British intelligence thought at the time. But it looks very much like a half-truth to me. The kinds of weapons which could be activated in forty-five minutes were relatively small battlefield ones and not the weapons of mass destruction which had dominated debate. Indeed, this is what the Intelligence and Security Committee, comprising members of parliament, concluded in its report, which exonerated Blair of the charge of lying, but said, 'The fact that it was assessed to refer to battlefield chemical and biological munitions and their movement on the battlefield, not to any other form of chemical or biological attack, should have been highlighted in the dossier.'

Half-truths exploit the difference between telling a lie and not telling the truth. One can fail to tell the truth by not saying everything, as well as by saying things that are false. But the idea that lies are of necessity ethically worse than half-truths is hard to defend. Indeed, given that it is not always wrong to tell a lie (as in the hackneyed example of lying to protect an innocent person from a potential killer) it seems what is crucial is intent and effect. And the effect and intent of a half-truth can be as good or bad, malicious or honourable, as that of a lie.

Rhetorically, however, half-truths can be more powerful than lies. Because half-truths are truths nonetheless, credible evidence can be given to support them. They can also be stated with total sincerity and conviction, just as long as the utterer is able to convince herself that, not being lies, they are really OK.

Imagining a world without half-truths is not easy. Think of all the unsaid, parenthetical qualifications we would need to make explicit in order to avoid any hint of *suggestio falsi*: reduced fat (but still high in it); I love you (but not in the way you want me to); your shirt is a nice colour (but what a terrible cut). There's a thin line between the benign white lie and the malign half-truth: where does it fall?

See also

71. What Sherlock didn't know

How else do you explain it?

> What the Psalmist said of himself is also true of us: 'Surely
> I was sinful at birth, sinful from the time my mother con-
> ceived me' (Psalm 51:5). And one sign of our sin is that we
> don't want God's way in our lives, and we are in rebellion
> against Him and His will. How else do you explain the evil
> in the world?
>
> Reverend Billy Graham[104]

Is a bad explanation better than no explanation at all? If your
coffee cup suddenly shatters for no apparent reason, and someone suggests it spontaneously gained consciousness, realized the
futility of its existence and committed suicide, would it be wise
to accept that explanation, provisionally at least, until a better
one was forthcoming?

Clearly there are some explanations which are worse than
no explanations at all. Yet humans don't seem comfortable living
with the unaccountable. We even talk of things themselves
'demanding an explanation', when really it is us doing the
demanding.

How else do you explain the rhetorical force of asking how
else you explain something? Asking a question like this shifts the
onus from the claim-maker to the person accepting or rejecting
the claim. Instead of having to provide evidence or arguments to

defend her position, the claim-maker is demanding that the person assessing her view either offers a better explanation or shuts up. But this shifting of onus is unreasonable. If you offer an explanation, it is up to you to show that it is a good one, not for me to show I have a better one. My rejection of your explanation does not require that I have a better one to hand. In the same way, if someone writes a terrible poem, it's no defence for them to argue that yours are worse.

This move is very often used by people whose views would otherwise seem outlandish to outsiders. Believers in the paranormal, for example, accept implausible explanations because they see them as the only way to dissolve the mysteriousness of various phenomena. In the absence of good explanations, they settle for crazy ones.

Billy Graham's use of the tactic is interesting in several respects. He skilfully combines plausible ideas acceptable to many with some more doctrinally specific ones. The idea that we are in some sense born with an inherent capability, or even tendency, to be selfish and do wrong is widely accepted. But he puts this idea together with concepts of separation from God, and sinfulness, so when he asks how else we explain evil in the world, one of the most obvious answers – that human beings are not intrinsically good – is already part of his own. In effect, it forces many people to, in part, agree with him, creating the impression that they don't have an alternative explanation at all.

Of course, in some sense, it is perfectly reasonable to ask what other explanations there could be. The key point is the spirit of the request. It can be part of a genuine search for answers: I'm at a loss here, I only have this rather poor explanation and I'd really appreciate a better one. But so often the real purpose is to make the lack of alternatives seem like a reason for accepting the one poor explanation being offered.

You may, however, remember something Sherlock Holmes said which is relevant: once you have eliminated all the other possibilities, the one that remains, however improbable, is the right one. That would be true, but only if we have indeed eliminated all other possibilities. The problem is that usually we have eliminated only the possibilities we happen to have thought of.

We cannot always suspend judgement, and sometimes the only explanation or course of action that seems at all plausible to us is unpalatable or bizarre sounding. If there are suspicious deaths happening and the only explanation you can think of is that your partner is the murderer, don't you have to act on that? 'How else can you explain it?' sometimes leads us to 'What else can I do?' In those situations, are bad explanations better than none at all, no matter what pure rational reflection tells us?

See also

72. Al Qaeda doesn't exist

Category mistakes

I get into trouble for saying that 'Al Qaeda' doesn't exist,
but there is no such organisation.

Peter Hitchens, *Mail on Sunday*[105]

The intelligentsia has never been keen on the war on terror,
often for good reasons. Its justified scepticism, however, has led
some to be too quick to dismiss every claim made by the
American and British governments. Both have been accused of
exaggerating the terrorist threat, sometimes by the same people
who, when Madrid and then London were both hit, claimed
that these attacks were inevitable.

One of these sceptical views is that Al Qaeda does not even
exist. But what does this claim boil down to? What it means is
that Al Qaeda is not a single, centrally run, global terrorist
organization. The attacks in New York, Madrid and London
were not all planned and directed by Osama Bin Laden and his
team. Rather, autonomous cells, which may have had no direct
contact with Bin Laden's group at all, organized these attacks on
their own.

To conclude, however, that Al Qaeda therefore does not
exist is as premature as saying that, for example, we cannot talk
about the French Resistance or Italian Partisans during the
Second World War. These resistance movements could not have

been tight, highly centralized movements with strict hierarchies. Rather, local groups often had to work more or less on their own. However, their shared goals and recognition of some kind of leadership mean it is often proper to talk about both movements in the singular.

Of course, it is possible to be confused by language and to assume that because we use singular nouns there must exist singular, discrete entities they refer to. But neither logic nor language demands that everything we talk of as a single entity is a simple, unified object. You might as well say that your love is not real unless it has determinate weight and dimensions.

The philosopher Gilbert Ryle argued that this false assumption was an example of what he called category mistakes. These occur when we think of one thing as though it were another kind of thing, and so misunderstand its nature. One of his most vivid examples is the tourist who demands to see Oxford University and is then puzzled when he is shown only colleges and libraries. He expected 'the university' to be a single building, not realizing that it was nothing more than the sum of its constituent parts.

Does this kind of Al Qaeda exist? In denying that it does, Peter Hitchens took his cue from Jason Burke's widely admired *Al Qaeda: The True Story of Radical Islam*. Burke, however, did not write a book about something that he didn't believe existed. Rather, as one reviewer put it, Burke's real thesis is that Al Qaeda *as we know it* does not exist, but that it is a 'formula system' for terrorism. This is significantly more than Hitchens's description of many groups 'vaguely linked by a common ideology'.

How then to avoid category mistakes? Perhaps all we need

do is remember an aphorism commended by Wittgenstein: 'Everything is what it is and not another thing.'[106]

To argue persuasively that someone has made a category mistake, you ought to be able to explain what kind of category the misdescribed entity really belongs in. You can't just say 'It's not that kind of stuff', you need to say what kind of stuff it actually is. So, for example, some theologians complain that scientistic atheists make a category mistake when they argue that, if the Catholic doctrine of transubstantiation were true, communion wine would literally turn into blood. 'The blood of Christ' does not belong in the same category as ordinary blood. But if that is so, what category does it belong in, and is it one where it makes sense to talk of 'blood' at all?

See also

10. Automorphism
39. False singulars
52. Failing to disaggregate
68. Missing the point

73. Ozone warming holes in the carbon layer

Blurring the boundaries

Air conditioning made it [global warming] all possible. And now having opened the door to southern pols and Dixie climes, it's also planning to export those hot summer winds all over the world by making the hole in the ozone layer a reality.

Michael Moore[107]

Ozone depletion and global warming are not two wholly unrelated issues. Both can be seen as examples of humankind's detrimental effects on the environment, and many ozone depleting chemicals are also greenhouse gases. But they are not as closely related as they are sometimes assumed to be.

Ozone depletion is mainly caused by chlorofluorocarbons (CFCs) and its main effect is to raise the amount of harmful ultraviolet B (UV-B) radiation reaching the Earth's surface. Global warming, on the other hand, is thought to be at least in part the result of increased man-made emissions of greenhouse gases such as carbon dioxide and methane, and its main effect is an increase in the Earth's temperature.

This has not stopped many people, often environmental campaigners, deliberately or otherwise, blurring the distinction between the two. In his polemic, for example, Michael Moore just seems to have got confused and taken ozone depletion to be a significant cause of global warming. But it isn't. (If there is a casual link it is probably the other way around: global warming could contribute to ozone depletion.) Moore has blurred the boundary which keeps the two issues distinct.

To understand any issue you need clarity and precision about all the important distinctions. You can't do that if you blur the boundaries of the debate. So why do it? Sometimes it is just ignorance. We lazily assume that two similar sounding issues must be more or less the same. Human beings are 'cognitive misers' who don't like to think about two things when we can get away with thinking about just one. This probably explains why too many people (although fewer by the day) have thought of smoking cannabis and injecting heroin as essentially the same kind of activity. It's much simpler to follow a rule like 'Legal drugs OK, illegal drugs bad' than it is to look at the wide range of different drugs available and analyse the similarities and differences between their effects, addictiveness, relation to crime and so on.

But sometimes the reasons for blurring the boundaries are more calculated. Blurring issues can be a useful rhetorical or polemical device. In the case of environmental campaigners, for instance, if ozone depletion and global warming are connected in people's minds, there is then a clear, single focus, rather than a messy web of vaguely related issues.

Boundaries have also been blurred between the war on terror and the conflict with Iraq. Any links between the two are indirect and probably more to do with long-term strategic aims (cutting off support for and dampening down militant Islam by instilling a Western-friendly, more or less secular regime in the heart of the Gulf) than the tactical hunt for Bin Laden and his supporters. But while it is true that there are some links between the two campaigns, it would have helped the Americans and British enormously if people had thought of the war in Iraq as a simple extension of the war on terror. Blurring the boundaries was thus intended as a means of increasing public support for the campaign in Iraq.

Sometimes, the accusation that an opponent is blurring the boundaries can itself be a rhetorical trick. Some issues really are messy and refusing to discuss them in a simple, atomistic fashion is a sign of wisdom, not slippery thinking. Ozone depletion and global warming; the war on terror and the Gulf war; soft and hard drugs: all these pairs of issues can be separated, but does that mean we are never right to link them?

See also

74. Everyone is bisexual

Low redefinition

Why do wars begin? The simple answer is that they never end.

Tom Palaima, professor of classics[108]

One of the most commented upon headlines in the world's press the day after 9/11 appeared in the liberal French newspaper *Le Monde*: 'We are all Americans'. It was a powerful expression of the solidarity of democrats everywhere in the face of an apparently new and terrifying threat.

No one who read it, however, would have been foolish enough to take it literally: the paper wasn't saying French citizens were entitled to US passports. We all understood that the usual sense of 'American' had been widened so that it carried a metaphorical and symbolic meaning, alongside its usual narrow one.

Yet the absurd move from the metaphorical to the literal can happen with a process known as low redefinition. This is when the legitimate meaning of a word is broadened in order to make a questionable proposition seem more plausible. It is so called because it lowers the bar for what can be described by the term.

This is what I think happened in Tom Palaima's argument about wars. He wanted to advance the thesis that war is essentially ceaseless. We ordinarily think about history as being divided between periods of peace and periods of war. In Western Europe, for example, it is thought that we have had peace since 1945, apart from a few regional conflicts, most notably those in the former Yugoslavia. Palaima, however, disputed this. War never ends, it simply goes through quieter and more active phases. 'Periods of so-called peace,' he wrote, 'were intervals when the competing nation-states were inevitably preparing for the next phase of open war.'

The problem with this thesis is that it is true only if war is understood in a broader sense than usual. It is not that we have been deceived about the absence of war in Western Europe, it is that there has not been war in the usual sense of the word. If you want to define war in a broader way, then you might be able to claim that war has never ceased. But we have to be clear that this requires a low redefinition of war – a broadening of its meaning – and is not just about correcting a false idea we have about it.

There may well be legitimate reasons for wanting such a low redefinition. In Palaima's case I think the motivating factor was a desire to make us reconsider the nature of peace. Palaima wanted to challenge the comfortable idea that, because battles have not been fought with great frequency in Western Europe since 1945, we live in a period of geopolitical calm and stability where military power is no longer an issue. Urging us to accept a low redefinition of war was a way of making this claim vivid.

Nevertheless, he did not make it explicit that he was revising our ordinary sense of war. So his *de facto* low redefinition of 'war' either fallaciously conflates the usual meaning of the word with his broadened one, in which case his argument is flawed; or it glosses over the revisionary nature of his claim, in which case his argument may be misleading.

Low redefinition is often more brazen. When people say 'chocolate is an addictive drug', 'everyone is bisexual' or 'altruism is ultimately just self-interest', they are in each case broadening the meaning of the central concepts to make what would otherwise be an outrageous claim plausible.

Low redefinition is particularly tempting in a culture which sees itself as democratic and egalitarian. Any term which excludes some people who might aspire to have it applied to them is prey to such revision. So, for example, in our culture the bar above which people qualify as 'celebrities' seems to have been lowered.

The advertising industry often uses of low redefinition to makes the ordinary sound extraordinary. My personal favourite is the wide use of 'passionate'. No matter what companies do, it seems they are passionate about it. This devalues the truly passionate, whose ardour is now put on a par with a corporate desire to make good curtain fittings. By the time you read this the award for most frequent use of a low-redefined word may have changed hands. Which would you nominate?

See also

75. Would you nuke the enemy?

No hypotheticals

I'm not going to answer hypotheticals.

Hillary Clinton[109]

Nigel Warburton dubbed the refusal to answer hypothetical questions the 'politician's answer', with good reason. It has become a favoured tool of evasion for politicians the world over. It is ironic that they are so keen to avoid hypothetical questions when their entire campaigns are run on the basis of hypotheticals: if you elect me, I'll do this. If they truly believed that they shouldn't answer hypothetical questions, then they should refrain from saying anything about what they would do if they gained power.

Although the mere fact that a question is hypothetical is no grounds for not answering it, there are good reasons why it is sometimes wise to keep schtum. You have to weigh up the probabilities of different outcomes, and their seriousness to decide whether in any given case 'We'll cross that bridge when we come to it' betrays a shocking lack of forethought (the plan for what to do in Iraq once Saddam had been toppled is a clear contender for this category) or a prudent conservation of intellectual energy (for instance, how to save tax in the 14 million to one chance that you win the lottery).

Another is that circumstances change, and it can be unwise

to commit yourself to a future course of action when unforeseen events may change the calculations about what the best course of action is. For example, before the Iraq war, Tony Blair frequently dodged the question of what he would do if there was no second UN resolution backing military action against Iraq. In this case, the existence or not of a UN resolution was just one of a number of factors which would contribute to his eventual decision. With events on the ground changing every day, unless you thought military action without UN backing was unjustifiable in all circumstances (in which case you would have to be opposed to the NATO action in former Yugoslavia and British intervention in Sierra Leone), Blair could not have predicted the eventual weighting the resolution, or lack of it, should have had in his deliberations.

But it is important to note that the problem here is not that the question about UN backing was hypothetical. It is rather that there were so many other variables that there was in fact no single hypothetical scenario in which UN backing was not forthcoming for Blair to comment on. Any number of different scenarios were consistent with that outcome, not all of which could even be foreseen, and all of which would have to be judged on their merits. Only if one already thought that the requirement for a UN resolution was absolute, which would make all the different scenarios identical in the one regard that mattered, could the hypothetical question be answered.

So what about the case of Clinton? She made her refusal after rival candidate Barack Obama said, 'I think it would be a profound mistake for us to use nuclear weapons in any circumstance.' When asked whether she agreed, she said, 'I'm not going to answer hypotheticals.' A poor defence by itself, but her fuller explanation made more sense. 'Presidents should be careful at all times in discussing the use and non-use of nuclear weapons,' she said. 'Presidents since the Cold War have used nuclear deterrents to keep the peace, and I don't believe any president should make blanket statements with the regard to use or non-use.'

The moral of the story is that though hypothetical questions often can and should be answered, sometimes they are justifiably met with silence. They have to be assessed on a case by case basis: there is no general rule as to whether they demand a reply.

Are there any hypothetical questions you believe it would be rash to try to answer? What would you do if you found out your partner had cheated on you; you were unable to work for some reason; or discovered your biological father was not who you thought he was? If your answer to any of these is 'it depends', then you can see why sometimes the politician's answer is not always such a shameless evasion after all.

See also

76. Why are we so stupid?

Fallacy of the complex question

What is it about what you do that is dangerous and why do people take exception to it?

Question to Peter Singer from Andrew Denton on
Enough Rope[110]

The standard example given to illustrate the fallacy of the complex question is 'When did you stop beating your wife?' Such a question asks one thing which assumes a second, when it is just this assumption which often needs to be established. First we need to know whether you did beat your wife. Only if it turns out that you did should we concern ourselves with when you stopped doing so.

The rhetorical power of a complex question is that any direct answer to it implicitly endorses the assumption, whereas any failure to offer a direct answer can look like an evasion. However, although in the heat of an argument it can throw someone off track, in this example and in another favourite – 'Why did you steal the money?' – it doesn't take much thought to see the trick and simply respond, 'I never started beating her' or 'I didn't steal the money'.

On his TV show *Enough Rope*, Andrew Denton posed a complex question to the controversial ethicist Peter Singer. 'What is it about what you do that is dangerous and why do people take exception to it?' Singer has certainly been called 'the most dangerous man on the planet', but a fairer question would have been to ask whether this is true, not what makes him dangerous.

Denton deliberately put the question in this provocative way because his is a fairly knockabout, light-toned show. It's a good example mainly for Singer's answer: 'I think that that particular epithet was because I've been a critic of what people sometimes call the "sanctity of life" view. That is, the view that every human life, just because it's human, is sacrosanct and must never be taken.' Singer did the only sensible thing one can do when faced with such a question – avoid a direct answer but address the real issues behind it. This shows there is at least one kind of situation where the question 'Why can't you give a straight answer' has a persuasive response.

The fallacy is harder to spot when people use a complex question rhetorically, not to make an accusation, but to frame a discussion or enquiry. In the *Guardian*, for example, the Reverend Giles Fraser opened an article by asking, 'Why are we so obsessed with what other people think of us? Why are we so concerned to fit in? Why do we submit so readily to the tyranny of the "they"?'[111] All three questions assume something that he has not established and which, on reflection, may well not be true of most of us. His questions encourage us simply to assume that we are all highly preoccupied with what other people think and to wonder only about why this should be so.

This kind of debate framing, which assumes a state of affairs which may not pertain, is remarkably common in the media. Often there is some flimsy basis offered, such as one report or single opinion poll. But then we are thrown straight into a debate: Why are people rejecting marriage? Why aren't British men romantic? Why can't actresses over forty get work? Why is the government destroying the BBC? How much freedom should we be prepared to sacrifice for security?

Which leaves me with one final puzzle: why do we fall for the fallacy of the complex question so easily?

People disagree about which assumptions a question can fairly make and which it cannot. What do you think of the following? Why are women still widely discriminated against in the workplace? Why is Sweden a better place to live than Portugal? Why aren't we doing enough to help the world's poor? Why is Italian pop music so awful?

See also

77. There's nothing lucky about luck

Fallacy of equivocation

If you master the art of being in charge of your own life and make the most of every situation that occurs, then you will attract more luck into your life.

Heather Summers and Anne Watson, *The Book of Luck*[112]

Wouldn't it be great to be luckier in life? Lucky like John Woods, who was not only scheduled to be on board the Pan Am flight that exploded above Lockerbie in 1988, but also left the World Trade Center on 11 September 2001 seconds before the building was struck by a hijacked aircraft.

Maybe you can. *The Book of Luck* promises to 'show you how to be lucky, always'. Too good to be true? Yes, as one of the authors freely admits. 'I believe that what we commonly consider to be luck is something that lies within our control,' says Anne Watson.[113] Confused? You should be. Indeed, I think the publishers are relying on your confusion. You see, there's luck and there's luck, and *The Book of Luck* is about luck, not luck, but it would help sales if you thought it were about the latter.

There are many words in our language that have multiple meanings. We commit the fallacy of equivocation when we use one word with two senses as if they had the same sense, and draw unjustified conclusions as a result. To take a somewhat absurd example, it is like arguing that cheese goes mouldy when it ages, Donald Trump is a big cheese who has aged, and so Donald Trump has gone mouldy. The words may be the same, but a 'big cheese' is not a big cheese.

In the same way, there is luck and there is luck. But in this case, the difference is not so glaringly obvious. The luck that Summers and Watson claim you can control concerns people's *perceptions* of their fortune and their tendency to succeed. They believe that this kind of luck has very little to do with random chance or the forces of destiny. Rather, people with a positive attitude, who persevere and take responsibility, will have more success. What we call luck in these cases is just the appearance or perception of luck, what we might call subjective luck.

This has nothing to do with another kind of luck, call it objective luck: luck around events and their consequences we have no control over. Summers and Watson are not so foolish to claim that being positive and persistent can protect you against this kind of bad luck, or bring you its good variant. No amount of positive thinking could have saved those above the ninety-third floor on the North Tower of the World Trade Center on 9/11, nor those on Pam Am Flight 103 on 12 December 1988.

Why then claim that you can 'attract more luck into your life' when you accept that what you mean by this isn't really luck at all? Whatever the answer to that – and I cannot read the authors' minds – this book certainly invites, even if it doesn't commit, the fallacy of equivocation. For instance, in one major newspaper article about the book, a journalist used the example of John Woods, conflating objective and subjective luck in just the way I believe the book and its website make it easy for you to do.

Another example is somewhat closer to home: do not assume that because someone is described as a 'popular philosopher' lots of people actually like him . . .

Many equivocations are deliberate and manipulative. When you're offered 'fresh' food at a café, should you conclude that it has been prepared on the spot from raw ingredients, or simply that it is not frozen? When politicians talk about how much they have increased (or reduced) spending, are they talking in real or absolute terms? And is it reasonable to think that a 'fast train' will actually travel quickly, rather than not stop at all the stations along the way? In my country, apparently not . . .

See also

78. It's only natural

The is/ought gap

'Hunting with hounds is the natural and most humane method of controlling the population of all four quarry species.

Over 500 members of the Royal College of
Veterinary Surgeons[114]

Fox-hunting has occupied a very peculiar role in British political life. Many people were baffled as to why this apparently barbaric practice was still going on at the turn of the century. The Labour Party had a long-term commitment to ban it, but it wasn't until nearly eight years after it came to power that it finally abolished hunting with hounds. For many others, however, the issue is not one of animal welfare, but of town versus country, or even simply of a kind of class hatred for the landed gentry who are the backbone of the hunting community.

Whatever the sociological undercurrents to the debate, the moral case against hunting rests on issues of animal welfare. It is therefore something of a challenge to opponents of hunting that over 500 members of the Royal College of Veterinary Surgeons claimed that hunting with hounds is the most humane method of controlling populations of foxes and other quarry species (such as deer, hare and mink). But does the additional claim that it is the natural method add anything to the hunters' case?

The fact that something is natural is just that: a fact (or perhaps we should say in this case, a hypothesis). What it is not is a verdict on the moral desirability of the practice. After all, it is more natural not to be anaesthetized than it is to be drugged into unconsciousness, but that does not mean performing medical operations without anaesthetic is morally preferable.

In fact, nothing about what *ought* to be the case follows from what actually *is* the case, natural or otherwise. This is known as the is/ought gap, first described by David Hume in his *A Treatise of Human Nature*. Hume's point is a simple logical one. For instance, if you want to reason from the fact that kicking people causes pain to the conclusion that you ought not kick people without good reason, you cannot do so unless you introduce a statement of values, such as 'causing pain without good reason is wrong'. You have to put values in to get values out: they are never simply generated from the facts.

The debate over the is/ought gap has become quite sophisticated and many philosophers argue that the gap is not unbridgeable. Even if they are right, a leap from facts to values with no demonstration of how this can happen is not justified.

Ignoring the is/ought gap is something that happens a lot when people look at human behaviour. It is sometimes claimed, for instance, that monogamy is unnatural, or that it is natural for men to be sexually predatory. Even if these claims are true, so what? Morality as normally understood surely sometimes requires us to go against our evolved predispositions. For example, many evolutionary psychologists would say that we have evolved to put the welfare of our close kin above that of strangers. But that would not make it right to favour a job application from a relative over a better-qualified stranger.

Of course, it is not the case that the is/ought gap (or the similar fact/value distinction) is so rigid that no matters of fact are relevant to matters of morality. Indeed, many facts are morally relevant. For instance, an acknowledgement that all human beings are of the same species is a powerful fact with which to confront certain breeds of racism. Facts may matter for values, but values cannot simply be read off from them.

On many occasions it just isn't obvious which facts matter for a moral position. Does the moral case against racial discrimination, for example, depend on the facts showing that there are no significant differences in factors such as IQ across different populations? Would innate differences between the sexes, if they could be shown to exist, change our attitudes to sexual discrimination? Do we need to know the facts about how animals experience pain in order to adjudicate on issues of animal welfare? Some of these facts are morally relevant, others are not. Which are which?

See also

79. The awful truth

It's terrible so it can't be true

> Only if God exists can there be purpose in life. The dilemma of modern man is thus truly terrible.
>
> William Lane Craig, theologian[115]

It is a sad fact about the world that just because many things are unpleasant, that doesn't mean they are not true. We all know this, and no sensible adult would accept the general principle that something's being unpalatable means that it is not the case. But however terrible it may be that people would argue like this, as a matter of fact, they do.

The fact of something's abhorrence is more often cited as good evidence for thinking that it can't be true, rather than as proof it can't be. For example, for months on end in 2007, the British media followed the story of Madeleine McCann, a three-year-old girl allegedly abducted from a holiday apartment in Praia da Luz, Portugal. Her parents soon became suspects in the case, and although dozens of children go missing every year, this story fascinated the media and the British public. It seemed everyone had an opinion as to whether the McCanns were guilty or innocent.

However, these verdicts were little more than speculation, since no one knew the full facts. That did not stop *Daily Mail* columnist Allison Pearson issuing her opinion: 'The deed the

McCanns are accused of would have required such black, cold-hearted evil that I refuse to believe they are guilty unless overwhelming evidence is uncovered.'[116]

Pearson did not go so far as to say that the terribleness of the alleged deed meant it could not have happened, but she still went too far. Sometimes parents do abuse and murder their own children. The fact that this is awful is not a good enough reason to believe it doesn't happen. The McCanns were official suspects, so the possibility that they did it was already a real one. They are, of course, innocent until proven guilty, and for what it's worth (not a lot) I don't think they did it either. But I can't see how the awfulness of the alleged crime in any way supports the case for their innocence.

The theologian William Lane Craig employs a similarly dubious line of argument when he claims that the 'absurdity of life without God' adds weight to the claim that God exists. This argument might work if the absurdity in question is some kind of logical one. But that's not what he means (at least not in the context in which I have quoted him). The absurdity he is talking about is similar to that discussed by Albert Camus, who argues that life is absurd without God but we must get on with it. It is absurd because it is meaningless and pointless.

But so what? Maybe life is meaningless and pointless. If it were (and I don't think that atheism necessitates this pessimistic conclusion) that may give you a reason for wanting God to exist, but that is not a reason to actually think he does. Sometimes terrible things are nonetheless true. In fact, often terrible things are nonetheless true.

But of course we often don't want to believe terrible things. This leads us into all kinds of self-deceptions. We don't want to believe that our partner is having an affair, so we discount all manner of evidence that they are. We don't want to believe that our close relatives and friends are capable of appalling crimes, which is why there is never any shortage of people willing to stand in front of television cameras to assert that someone charged with a crime 'could never have done it'.

As T. S. Eliot famously said, 'Humankind cannot bear very much reality.' We cannot expect people always to stare the truth in the face fearlessly, even though we might aspire to such heroism. It may be terrible that people are unable to accept terrible things, but it is surely also true that sometimes they can't. How much should we resist this unpalatable fact of human nature?

Arguably, several major philosophical theories have proven unpopular mainly because they are so unpalatable, not because the arguments for them are weak. This raises a further question of whether what we think would be awful, if true, really would be that bad. Would it be terrible to believe that human beings lacked ultimate free will? Could we accept that what we think does not actually cause us to do what we do? And would it be the end of decency if there were no objective moral values?

See also

80. Balancing fudge

'We have to strike a balance'

We've got to strike a balance between enabling people to travel and meeting our environmental obligations.

Alistair Darling, transport secretary[117]

'Let's be reasonable.' That's an appeal surely no one would reject. Who would suggest being unreasonable? But that's the problem: it's such a vague aspiration. Its main function seems to be to make whoever utters it sound like a, well, reasonable kind of person.

'Striking a balance' is a similarly woolly and platitudinous thing to do. No one is going to say, 'I think that in assessing the evidence, we should strive to be unbalanced.' Whenever there are competing arguments, or lists of pros and cons, there is a need to balance them out. Doing so is what thinking about things entails: striking a balance is not some extra activity that rational deliberation can avoid.

Talk of striking a balance is thus empty unless it explains to us just what balance has to be struck and why. Yet this is rarely what happens when people evoke the phrase. Rather, they simply throw it in as an apparent justification for a decision that seems to avoid making tough choices.

This is what Alistair Darling, the then transport secretary, was doing in his interview with Andrew Marr. The tough question was how we can reduce CO_2 emissions while having as little impact on economic growth as possible. To say 'We've got to strike a balance between enabling people to travel and meeting our environmental obligations' does not answer this tough question at all, it merely restates the challenge of providing a decent answer. A genuine answer would be something like 'In order to meet our environmental obligations, we have to stop people travelling so much' or 'It is worth compromising on some of our environmental objectives to allow people to travel freely.' But, of course, both answers involve accepting something unpalatable. Safer then just to talk the language of striking a balance, even if it would be more accurate to say that what's been struck is a fudge.

Talk of balance can be reassuring when, in fact, what is needed is a radical rebalancing of priorities. On green issues, it may be that we cannot simply hope to maintain current levels of carbon consumption. On that analysis, it would be false and dangerous to promote the idea that somehow we can balance the urgency of action against climate change with the maintenance of many habits and practices we have got used to.

Alas, 'We have to strike a balance' now seems to be the stock answer to any hard questions about environmental policy. For instance, in the House of Lords, the Labour peer Lord Davies of Oldham was asked how a new tax aimed at reducing the carbon emissions of aeroplanes squared with the decision to approve a second runway at Stansted airport. His answer was, of course, 'We have to strike a balance between our environmental objectives.'[118]

What's worse is that the apparent reasonableness of balance blinds us to the fact that, sometimes, one set of concerns just overrides the other. Consider the balance that we are told needs to be struck between security and civil liberties. In the abstract, there is some truth in this claim. But in some specific policy areas, the right balance might mean tilting the scales entirely to one side. There is, for instance, arguably no balance that needs to be struck between incarcerating people without trial for years on end and national security; the former just should not happen. No balancing is required when the scales come firmly down on one side.

Many debates come down to much harder choices that the rhetoric of balance avoids. For instance, is the ethics of abortion really about striking a balance between the rights of the mother and those of the foetus? Should national health services balance the provision of clinically tested procedures and other, complementary therapies? Must we balance the opinions of racists and bigots against those of others?

See also

81. I've brought you peace and prosperity!

Taking the credit

> This year we celebrate the fiftieth anniversary of the European Union. We are proud of this achievement, which has brought peace, prosperity and solidarity to a continent wracked by war.
>
> José Manuel Barroso, president of the European Commission[119]

What do you want from your government? You can't ask for much more than peace and prosperity, can you? Well, according to its president, that's just what the European Union has given its member states. Three cheers for the EU then?

Not so fast. It is true that there have been no wars between the EU's member states since it was founded, though there had been plenty in the centuries before. It is also true that Europe is now pretty rich, richer than it was when the EU started. But the claim that the EU has actually been the cause of this peace and prosperity requires more evidence than the statement of these two facts.

Consider, for instance, how many countries outside the EU in Europe have also done pretty well on the peace and prosperity front. Most notably, Norway has the second highest GDP per capita in the world, and has also regularly topped the UN's Human Development Index chart, making it the best place to live in the world. Who is to say that other countries in the EU would not have had similar success if the union had never been created?

Politicians like to take the credit for what goes well, just as they like to avoid the blame for what goes wrong. In that, they are only human. In his 2003 Labour Party Conference speech, for example, the then prime minister, Tony Blair, proudly cited the reduction in cancer deaths under the watch of his government. He did not point out that the long-term trend throughout the developing world is for such a reduction and Britain's 9 per cent drop was only in line with European averages. At best his government performed only averagely, and arguably had little direct control over the medium- to long-term trends at all.

As a rhetorical move, taking the credit can be effective, partly because humans instinctively understand the world as operating according to causal principles, and it's a good job that we do. But the downside of this is that we can easily mistake non-causal conjunctions for causal ones. Success under a certain regime is thus easily mistaken for success because of a regime.

Unfairly taking the credit (or the blame) in such manner is not restricted to the political sphere. Consider the implied causal claims in the following: 'Since we've been married, your career has shot ahead, while mine has stagnated.' Or, 'There has not been a single fatality in this factory all the time I've been the manager.' Or how about, 'The man who won five of the six major championships played between August 1999 and April 2001 with Titleist equipment has won only two of the last seven, and none of the last five, with the Nike driver in the bag.' That man was Tiger Woods, and that statement was made during his lean spell. He has since gone on to recover his pre-eminence in his sport, with Nike clubs. Could it just simply be that neither Nike nor Titleist should take the credit for his success, and that Woods is simply a brilliant sportsman who has his ups and downs?

That said, I'm sure that if this books sells well it will be down to my skill and hard work, and if it flops it will be the publisher's fault.

Just as people unfairly take the credit, so the same lack of clarity about cause and effect can lead to some not getting the recognition they are due. Tony Blair may have claimed more successes than he should have, but do his critics deny him his actual achievements? Was Alan Greenspan a brilliant chairman of the Federal Reserve or just a lucky one? Is it even possible to determine how much credit people should really get, or is the effect of chance too great to make any such judgements meaningful?

See also

82. A sharp tongue does not mean a keen mind

Ad hominems

> I could endure Irving's possessing the most embar-
> rassingly malodorous breath in London, because he
> provided access to people and material of historical
> importance.
>
> Max Hastings, *Guardian*[120]

Here's a scene everyone is familiar with: two people are having a debate, and one of them is getting very wound-up by the other. At this point, the interlocutor with the upper hand says something particularly smart, to which the other person has no coherent response. So, instead, he says, 'That's what I'd expect a stupid **** like you to say.' (Interactive feature: insert your own expletive.)

This is a paradigmatic example of an *ad hominem* argument. *Ad hominem* attacks do not address the substance of an argument but the people making them. As such, they're obviously rationally deficient, though often quite entertaining.

Max Hastings's remark about historian David Irving is an unusual example because in the context in which he uttered it he was defending Irving, saying that for all his faults as a holocaust denier, he unearths information of great importance to historians. 'No serious historian of the Second World War can exclude Irving's books from the reading list,' said Hastings. So why the insult?

Well, Irving is a pariah in polite society, so presumably Hastings thought being rude about him might help make it clear that his qualified support for some of his historical work is in no way an endorsement of him as a human being. The tactic probably worked: no one who read Hastings's barbed put-down could think any love was lost between him and Irving. It was a neat rhetorical trick which told us nothing about the merits of Irving as an intellectual.

However, we should not throw the baby out with the bath water: a good insult need not be a mere *ad hominem*. Indeed, the best cut deeper. Consider, for example, William Faulkner's comment about Ernest Hemingway: 'He has never been known to use a word that might send a reader to the dictionary.' It's an insult yes, but is it a mere *ad hominem*? Not at all: Faulkner is trying to tell us something about the deficiency of the work, not just the man. The proof of this is that, allowing for a bit of overstatement, Faulkner's claim can be tested, and we can ask ourselves whether or not this amounts to a failing in Hemingway's work. In contrast, whether or not David Irving has bad breath does not alter the quality of his history one bit.

There is one remark I recently heard which I think merits inclusion in any list of great put-downs which, again, was much more than an *ad hominem*. After being introduced at length, the speaker remarked that, as ever, the chair had delivered a talk 'which is a tough act to follow – in every sense of the word'. In a way, the remark was wasted, because, actually, the introduction had been perfectly clear. But even philosophers (as both speakers were) agree that the truth should never get in the way of a good joke.

For different reasons, another favourite example of mine comes from the Reverend Ian Paisley. He mocked the journalist Deborah Ross, who had the temerity to ask him to justify his claim that he knew what God thought. 'A silly girl asked me today how I knew what God thought,' Paisley told an Orange Lodge meeting, 'and I had to say to her I know because it is written in the Bible.'[121] What's interesting here is that he answered Ross's question ('It is written in the Bible'). His *ad hominem* remark about her alleged stupidity pre-emptively dismissed the validity of the obvious follow-ups, such as why he thinks his scriptural interpretation is superior to that of the Pope, or how he knows the Bible is God's word.

Ross had the last laugh though: her brilliant write-up of the interview made Paisley look like the silly one. *Ad hominems* can easily backfire if they make the attacker look irrational and vicious.

It is not always obvious when an insult is purely personal and when it contains some sort of serious criticism constitutive of a rational argument. What do you make of Elizabeth Bowen's description of Aldous Huxley: 'The stupid person's idea of a clever person'? Or Gore Vidal's verdict on Andy Warhol: 'The only genius with an IQ of 60'? Or what about Mamie Van Doren's acidic remark about Warren Beatty: 'He's the type of man who will end up dying in his own arms'? Mere *ad hominems* or insults that pack an intellectual punch?

See also

83. Tooled up, obviously

Appeals to common sense

> This is a classic example of us just applying some common sense, just being reasonable, right? And reasonable would say that lawful gun owners – I respect the Second Amendment – I think lawful gun owners should be able to hunt, be sportsmen, protect their families.
>
> Barack Obama[122]

For politicians, appealing to common sense is, well, common sense. It's something that everyone thinks they have in abundance, although intellectual elites are often said to lack it. It's democratic, simple and self-evident, so who would want to argue against it? Me. Common sense is a poor indicator of what is true, or for those who are suspicious of the 'T' word, of what is reliable, practical or efficacious.

This point was made forcibly in the biologist Lewis Wolpert's book *The Unnatural Nature of Science*.[123] Wolpert points out that science repeatedly confounds common sense, or at the very least what is seen as common sense at any particular time. For example, common sense held that a heavy object would fall faster than a light one. Common sense would say that if the world were a sphere, people would fall off, and we'd definitely be propelled into space if the world were spinning. Common sense – or at least received wisdom – says that going out into the cold in wet clothes increases your chances of getting a cold. Common sense on all three counts is wrong.

It doesn't take much to show that common sense is unreliable. Yet I too find the lure of common sense almost irresistible. An appeal to common sense is often an expression of a kind of exasperation. Something seems obviously true or false to us and we really don't think it is worth the effort of explaining why. Invoking common sense is thus just a shorthand way of saying we think something is obviously true or false. It's a misleading strategy, since 'common sense' implies a kind of universal standard of rationality. It is more than just what ordinary people happen to think, but requires less than specialized knowledge. But if it is more than mere received opinion, doesn't it simply become what we believe people ought to think? And if this is what we mean when we talk about common sense, shouldn't we say so and make clear why we think they ought to agree with us? Saying it is just common sense is a way of shifting responsibility for having to explain why we think what we do onto some mythical judge of ordinary reason.

So common sense is not just unreliable, it's hazy and ill-defined. We should try to avoid using the phrase altogether and instead replace it with something that at least makes the basis of our judgement clear: it is what people generally think; it is what all experience points to being true; it is received wisdom; it is what I think is obvious; it is self-evident. Not all of these are good justifications for belief. But at least they are clear and make it possible to assess honestly what the justifications are. Saying something is common sense is just a way of trying to avoid justifying it altogether.

Has common sense got any defence against this charge sheet? I think it has. There are countless examples of where our unreflective, intuitive responses get it right quicker or more accurately than our more systematic deliberations. Common sense can also embody a kind of collective wisdom, rules of thumb which usually work and are justified by the tribunal of history, not rational argument. The trouble is that it is hard to distinguish this perfectly good variety of common sense from widely accepted falsehoods.

Common sense may be dubious, but gratuitously denying it is a cheap way of sounding intellectual. I've devised a game called Žižuku – named after the Slovenian cultural theorist and top player Slavoj Žižek – which allows you to dazzle others with your intellect this way. Just take anything that is widely believed and invert it, preferably to create a wise-sounding paradox. For example, 'The more we use psychology to make us feel happier, the more miserable we become.' Or, 'It is the obsession with "healthy eating" which is actually making us unhealthier.' More controversially, 'Anti-racism is the most racist thing of all, because it, above all else, objectifies race.' Now, your turn . . .

See also

84. Hamburger heroin

False analogies

> For a large number of people, a steady diet of fast food is almost as harmful and as difficult to resist as heroin is to an addict or nicotine is to a habitual cigarette smoker.

John Banzhaf, attorney and law professor[124]

Several lawsuits have already been filed against fast-food restaurants claiming that they are responsible for the ill health of the obese who have fed for years on their products. Although many people regard them as a kind of joke, some class action suits have even been successful.

Before John Banzhaf started fighting the fast-food corporations, he was one of those who sued 'big tobacco'. People ridiculed these attempts too, but in 1998, the Master Settlement Agreement saw the major US tobacco companies agree to pay $246 billion over twenty-five years to settle lawsuits filed by US states.

The success of the tobacco suits has led people to ask if claims made against junk-food manufacturers are analogous. In both cases, it is claimed that public health has been damaged by the actions of major corporations who concealed the health risks of their products. This makes them liable to pay damages to those who suffered as a result.

From a legal point of view, there are certainly precedents set by the tobacco suits which those pursuing fast-food manufacturers will want to learn from. But are the two cases truly analogous?

One legitimate way to draw an analogy in an argument is to identify a common logical structure. For example, it can be argued that the arguments against the tobacco and fast-food industries have the same form, namely:

1. If a manufacturer covers up the harm its products can cause, it is responsible for any such harm its products do cause.
2. X has covered up the harm its products can cause.
3. Therefore X is responsible for any such harm its products have caused.

If (1) is true, then X can be substituted for anything which makes (2) true and the conclusion (3) will follow. In this way, the two arguments are indeed analogous. In fact, they both share a basic valid form known as affirming the antecedent:

If P then Q
P
Therefore Q

However, the fact that arguments against big tobacco and the fast-food industry have the same structure is not in itself very interesting. What we need to know is whether the *content* of the arguments is analogous, not just the *forms*. Has the fast-food industry engaged in a health cover-up comparable to that of the tobacco companies?

This is where the analogy might break down. First, if you smoke, any harm you suffer is unavoidable; if you eat fast food, harm comes only from misuse. It should have been obvious to tobacco companies a long time ago that their products were intrinsically damaging to health. Warnings such as those now placed in adverts by the alcohol industry – 'use our product responsibly' – would be absurd on cigarette packets. But fast food, like alcohol, can be enjoyed in moderation without harm to health.

More critically for the argument we have looked at, in the case of smoking there seemed to be a clear cover-up; in the case of fast food, it would be hard to demonstrate such grave deception. The facts about what constitutes a healthy diet have been sufficiently known for enough time. It is therefore possible to make the case that consumers should have been able to choose for themselves how much fast food they consumed. The same was not true of smoking.

Arguments from analogy can be rhetorically powerful, but it is vital we question whether the parallels are close enough to justify the conclusions drawn from them.

What do you make of these arguments from analogy? For example, is 'speciesism' against animals comparable to racism or sexism? Are hard-line atheists as fundamentalist as religious zealots who advocate killing in God's name? Are fake boobs the same kind of thing as fake tans? What exactly is being compared in each case, and how close is the similarity?

See also

85. Fear of black pepper

Scaremongering

> More than 50 dangerous pesticides contaminate Britain's food, official tests reveal. [. . .] The revelation – in a survey of official testing results – will heighten concern about food contamination.
>
> Geoffrey Lean, *Independent on Sunday*[125]

Geoffrey Lean, the former environment editor of the *Independent on Sunday*, should not be a soft target for criticism. He has won numerous prizes, including a special award for lifetime achievement in environmental journalism from the World Conservation Union, the Martha Gellhorn Prize, the Reuters-IUCN Media Award and the British Press Award Scoop of the Year. Yet finding faults in his report on the 'more than 50 dangerous pesticides found in British food' is like shooting fish in a barrel. Big fish. In a small barrel. With a machine gun.

Lean's piece uses a classic scaremongering move: it points to the existence of a risk while downplaying or not even revealing the fact that the risk in question is extremely low. An obvious example of the dodgy nature of this move is the lightning rod marketer who turns up and says to you, 'Did you know your house – yes, *your* house – could be struck by lightning tomorrow, causing a fire which could kill you and all your family? Do you want to take that risk?'

Your answer would probably be 'yes', because you already know that your house could be struck by lightning, but you also know the risk is so low it's not worth spending lots of money to avoid it. However, when someone confronts you with a risk you weren't aware of, all this background information is not there, and the natural reaction is to be concerned. 'Did you know your saucepans could give you Alzheimer's?' Well, no, I didn't. Gosh. Perhaps I should buy some safe ones . . .

When Lean tells us that British food contains 'dangerous pesticides' without revealing their levels, he is making us more scared than we need be. It is like telling someone there is arsenic in the glass of water they have just drunk, when there is no more than a trace of the poison, not enough to have any significant effect on their body. Yet nowhere in his piece does Lean point to evidence that the levels of these pesticides are dangerously high.

Astonishingly, Lean actually pre-empts this criticism by claiming that 'Many experts believe that there is no safe level for a cancer-causing chemical.' In other words, you should be scared by the mere presence of the harmful pesticides, irrespective of how low their levels are. But this claim is either patently false or not quite what it seems. For example, black pepper has been found to be a carcinogen, as have tannins, which are found in tea and coffee. Yet no credible expert believes that it is not safe to drink tea or grind black pepper on your pasta. You just wouldn't be able to consume the quantities of these foodstuffs required for their carcinogenic effects to kick in.

This kind of frankly irresponsible reporting also allows the reporter to make a self-fulfilling prophesy. 'The revelation . . . will heighten concern,' wrote Lean. Well, yes it will, because he's revealed it in a way designed to heighten concern. Nothing spreads fear like telling people that fear is spreading.

Try this experiment: pick up almost any newspaper today and look for stories that warn of risks, any risks: house price crashes, global disaster, terrorist attack, poisoning, whatever. I bet you that in almost all cases the story will stress the mere presence of the risk and not its actual level. The result is that we are made more worried than we should be, but without anyone actually lying. The sin here is a sin of omission, but sometimes it is what you don't say that can be deceptive.

See also

86. There is no dark side of the moon

The power of bold assertion

> Think about it: every time there's a list of the 100 greatest records of all time, all those albums were recorded in two days.
>
> Jack White of The White Stripes[126]

Think about it? This is the twenty-first century! Why think when you can Google? A search for 'greatest records of all time' will take you to *Rolling Stone*'s readers' poll, in which you'll find such classics as *Sgt Pepper's, OK Computer, Dark Side of the Moon* and, er, *Achtung Baby*. Top of their poll was the Beatles' *Revolver*. It's a familiar selection, reflected in countless other polls and surveys. Among musicians and music writers, certain albums tend to do even better, notably the Beach Boys' *Pet Sounds*, a perennial critics' favourite.

Revolver was not recorded in two days. In fact, it was recorded over eight weeks and, like *Sgt Pepper's*, is considered by many to be a landmark album precisely because of the innovative and extensive use of technology, mixing and production in the studio. Brian Wilson spent four months recording just the backing tracks for *Pet Sounds*. The recording of *Dark Side of the Moon* took place between June 1972 and January 1973. *OK Computer* took several months, spread over a couple of years, to record. Need I go on? Jack White is plain, demonstrably, wrong.

Getting your facts wrong is such a basic mistake that it barely registers as a bad argumentative move. Yet it is probably one of the most common and easily missed. Goebbels said that 'If you tell a lie big enough and keep repeating it people will eventually come to believe it.' He could equally have said that if you state an untruth boldly and confidently enough, people are remarkably willing to accept what you say. This, incidentally, is a major problem with relying too much on eye-witness testimony in court. Psychology experiments have shown that witnesses who are most confident about their recollections are both the most likely to be believed and the least likely to be accurate in their reports.

It seems that unless we have a particular reason to doubt the truth of a claim, we tend to assume it is right. And it would indeed be difficult to be sceptical about everything we hear which we don't know for sure to be true. 'Innocent until proven guilty' is the principle that allows us to get on with our lives without having constantly to stop and question.

However, what is most striking about the power of bold assertion is that it can make us accept things which even the briefest reflection would show to be false. You have to think only for a moment about what the so-called greatest records of all time are to realize straight away that very few were recorded in just a couple of days. But faced with a confidently made claim, we often don't think, we just accept.

Nor should we comfort ourselves with the thought that we would be more cautious when the subject is more serious than the top 100 albums. We often accept uncritically the things people say, particularly if we admire or support them, just as groundlessly as we dismiss claims made by their critics.

We usually have to accept things are true just as long as they sound plausible and we have no particular reason to doubt them. Operating by those principles works most of the time and saves us a lot of time and trouble. For instance, did you know whether my earlier claim about the reliability of eye-witness testimony was right or not? If not, did you get suspicious of it, or check it? Taking a certain amount on trust is unavoidable, but it makes it all too easy for people, deliberately or not, to take advantage of our tendency not to question simple assertions.

Researchers at Cardiff University recently looked at 2,000 news stories in serious British newspapers and found that 80 per cent were wholly, mainly or partially based on second-hand material, and the key facts had been checked in only 12 per cent of them.[127] Try your own, less scientific, version of this study. For one day, ask of every factual claim you hear or read whether you can really trust that it is true. I'd bet that the answer will often be no, and that the task will quickly become exhausting.

See also

1. Arguments from incredulity
20. It worked for me . . .
31. Arguments from authority
47. *Argumentum ad fatigum*

87. If it's not all bad it must be all good

Partial defence ≠ support

> In the *Guardian* last week, the eminent philosopher Julian Baggini announced that, contrary to appearances, New Labour's plans for identity cards were an idea which should be embraced by the left.
>
> Nick Cohen, *Observer*[128]

Bad argumentative moves can be made by readers as well as writers. When those readers are writers themselves, the result can be flagrant misrepresentation of someone's position, which is very irksome for the inaccurately portrayed party.

I have been at the receiving end of this kind of thing several times now, and a pattern seems to be emerging. Time and again, people mistake a partial defence of something for full support of it. It seems impossible to point out that something can be said for x or y without someone who should know better interpreting that as meaning that, on balance, you think x or y is a good thing.

For example, someone on the widely respected *Crooked Timber* blog attacked a column in my Bad Moves series for the Butterflies and Wheels website, saying 'the whole argument was undermined by the blatant political stance of the writer'. What he then went on to say was true 'according to Baggini' just wasn't what I had said at all. What seems to have happened is that he saw that I had, *on one specific point*, defended Blair and criticized one of his opponents, and he had therefore assumed that I *in general* supported Blair: a classic example of mistaking a partial defence for full support.

Nick Cohen made the same mistake. In a *Guardian* article, I had tried to argue that the debate over compulsory ID cards in the UK was dominated by concerns about limits on freedom from government 'interference'. Discussion had neglected questions about how far government involvement in our daily lives can increase our freedom to act.

Whether or not my argument was a good one, I quite clearly stopped short of recommending ID cards, saying that I suspected the measure would not 'reap a big enough dividend in terms of increasing our positive freedom to go about our business safely' and describing the plan as 'half-baked'. But it seems this was not clear enough. Partially defending the home secretary David Blunkett and seeing some merit in the grounds of his arguments was quickly confused with being a supporter of him and his measures.

Cohen was perhaps being deliberately mischievous. After all, his description of me as an 'eminent philosopher' was an ironic in-joke. (He had used the term previously in an openDemocracy exchange and, when I corrected him, he made 'an unreserved apology' saying 'I withdraw the slur at once and promise never to repeat it.')

I suspect people confuse partial defences for full support so easily because of the desire to divide the world into clearly opposing camps – 'us' and 'them'. If you tend to think in this way, partial defences can look like signs and signals of what someone really believes. In such a binary world, for me to admit that Blair or Blunkett has a point is therefore a sign that I'm a closet authoritarian Blairite. Maybe I am! But the partial defences I have described show no such thing, for I have also partially defended the political opponents of these people and I can't be a closet supporter of everyone.

There are certain areas of debate where the leap to polarization seems to be made more easily. Is it not the case that, in the US, someone who expresses support for the Palestinian right to self-determination is often labelled an anti-Semite? Meanwhile, in the UK, defending certain aspects of Israeli policy will get you labelled as a neo-Zionist.

This kind of error is widespread. As well as trying to put others straight, we should ask ourselves to what extent we jump to conclusions about what the partial support given by others really says about their wider beliefs.

Most of us seem to find it very hard to see any merit in the views of people we generally disagree with. So try every now and again to see what of genuine merit could be said in favour of a view you strongly disagree with. As well as finding it difficult, you might also feel a visceral, emotional resistance to this exercise in intellectual empathy.

See also

88. If it's old it's good

Fallacy of ancient wisdom

> If we do not act, if we become silent, governments will be
> free to replace the teachings of all ages with toxic lies.
> Timeless natural medicines, foods and herbs with which
> we have evolved, culled from thousands of years of col-
> lected wisdom, will be swept way, crushed under the
> myopic weight of corporate greed.
>
> Dame Judi Dench, actor[129]

If you don't want to be crushed by the wheels of the pharma-
ceutical industry, here's what Dame Judi says you must do:
oppose the Codex Alimentarius, an international set of rules on
food safety which the World Trade Organisation uses to settle
trade disputes. This codex has been used to control the sale of
food supplements and herbal medicines. This, apparently, is a
bad thing, because it reduces our 'health freedom' and leaves us
reliant on dangerous modern medicines.

When deciding whether or not to heed Dame Judi's call to
balms, there is one thing no sensible person should do: fall for
the myth that the age of a practice or remedy is in any way
indicative of its effectiveness.

Dench appeals to the age of remedies as though this is some
kind of recommendation. She talks of 'teachings of all ages',
'timeless natural medicines' and 'thousands of years of collected

wisdom'. Ironically, though, one of the main things opponents of the codex want to protect are vitamin pills, a twentieth-century invention.

It should be enough just to point out that 'it's been done for centuries, therefore it must be good' is a simple *non sequitur*. If anything, the old age of a treatment is a reason to be suspicious of it, since centuries ago there was little or no understanding of how the human body worked and people routinely died from what are now seen as minor illnesses. It would be quite incredible if such biologically and medically undeveloped cultures were the source of many effective remedies.

Indeed, our love of old therapies is extremely selective. Blood-letting dates back to the fifth century BCE and probably owes its origins to Hippocrates. It is based on the discredited principle that the human body needs to maintain a balance between its four 'humours': blood, phlegm, yellow bile and black bile. Like many horrific medical practices of old, it has rightly been consigned to history (even, presumably, by Judi Dench), not before its misguided application killed off George Washington, among others.

So what is it about ancient wisdom that makes it so attractive? When it comes to Eastern practices, one reason is surely the mythologizing about the East that is common in Western society. Places such as China, Tibet and India are seen as very 'spiritual', as though the people there were not made of flesh and blood like the Americans, French and British.

A more promising reason is that these remedies have been 'tried and tested'. It is intuitively plausible that if something has endured for centuries, there must be something in it. But on that logic, there must be something in slavery and the inequality of women.

Of course, it is crass to go completely the other way and insist that no ancient wisdom can be true and that only the modern has value. Many herbs have been found to have therapeutic qualities, although even here some modern medicines may still be more effective. The key, however, is that they are held to be effective because they have been properly tested, not because they are old and therefore have somehow been tried and tested by history.

In order to distinguish between ancient wisdom and outdated non-sense, you can't afford to be prejudiced either way. Old ideas can persist for good and bad reasons. Why is the institution of marriage so durable? Why do women still find it hard to rise to the top of their professions? Why hasn't God died, as many secular humanists insisted he would? Why do people still eat meat? Is the persistence of all marriage, gender inequality, belief in God and carnivorousness a reflection of the ancient wisdom that has made them part of our societies for centuries, or should they be thrown on the scrapheap of history, like blood-letting, witch-hunting and feudalism?

See also

89. The voyeur's charter

'The innocent have nothing to fear'

> If a government takes offence at this, that government should be offended by the acts of its own citizens, if they are hateful.

Lynne Weil, US State Department communications director[130]

Alarmed by an apparent rise in anti-Semitism, especially in Europe, in 2003 the US Congress decided that the situation needed monitoring and ordered the State Department to 'start rating governments throughout the world on their treatment of Jewish citizens'.

Several countries, however, objected to this. But State Department communications director Lynne Weil argued that there were no good reasons for any government to object to such reporting. In essence, her argument was that if a country had no particular problem with anti-Semitism, then nothing in the reports would be objectionable to them. But if they did have a problem, then they should be concerned not with the reporting, but with the problem. Only anti-Semitic nations had anything to worry about, and quite rightly so.

This is a version of the very popular 'The innocent have nothing to fear' argument, which is wheeled out whenever authorities wish to bring in new measures which increase surveillance or limit freedoms in the name of increasing security.

For example, someone demands to search your luggage. You object to this intrusion on your privacy, but you are told that if you are innocent, you have no reason to object. After all, what are you trying to hide?

The argument is a particular species of false dichotomy. You are presented with a simple either/or choice. Either you're guilty, and so should be exposed; or you are innocent, in which case nothing will be exposed, and therefore you have nothing to worry about. Either way, you have no legitimate reason to be concerned. Like all false dichotomies, the problem is that there is at least one more option than the two offered in the either/or choice.

In the case of 'The innocent have nothing to fear' argument, the legitimate riposte is usually that our objections have nothing to do with our guilt or innocence but with our right to privacy. Consider, for example, that what we get up to in our bedrooms may be nothing to be ashamed of, but most of us still wouldn't want others to stand around and watch. Potential voyeurs would not have a very strong case if they simply said, 'Why not let us look? Doing something you shouldn't be?' 'The innocent have nothing to fear' is therefore usually an example of a red herring: the fact that we are not doing anything wrong is beside the point.

Lynne Weil's argument is a red herring for a slightly different reason. It was not privacy violation that foreign governments objected to, but what they saw as the particular focus on anti-Semitism as opposed to other forms of discrimination. State Department diplomats warned that the measures would open up the US government to charges of favouritism: focusing on anti-Semitism more than other, perhaps more widespread, forms of discrimination and oppression. Whether that is a good argument is of course another matter. However, since this was the official basis of the concern, Lynne Weil's response clearly misses the point. What the innocent fear is not being found out, but living under an intrusive or unjust regime.

'The innocent have nothing to fear' can be a legitimate point to make if what it really means is 'The fears expressed by the innocent are unfounded.' The difference is subtle but important. For example, in the UK there has been a long-running debate over the introduction of ID cards. Some of the objections to this revolve around worries that people have about how their data will be used. If these worries were unfounded, the innocent would have nothing to fear, and explaining why would be relevant.

You may be worried that an internet social networking site might share your data with others; that laws to allow detention of terror suspects without charge will give the police too much power; that speed cameras effectively track your movements around the country. In some of these cases, it might be true that the innocent have nothing to fear in that nothing bad will happen to them as a result. But does that mean these fears of the innocent are unfounded and can be dismissed?

See also

90. How can I ever believe you again?

Arguments from fallibility

Why should anyone believe another word the politicians or government scientists say? After all that has happened, can there be the slightest confidence in official reassurances about the supposed safety of GM foods?

Daily Mail[131]

In December 2007 the *Mail* issued an apology and paid undisclosed damages after falsely reporting that two men had run a fraudulent and dishonest business. In August of the same year, it paid more than £45,000 in legal costs and issued an apology to a Sikh police officer it falsely accused of racism. In June it had to apologize to a man it falsely accused of being the criminal mastermind behind a £53 million robbery, and again paid damages. In the same month it paid £5,000 libel damages to a Labour MP it falsely accused of delivering a foul-mouthed outburst to a security guard.[132] Worst of all, it once gave one of my books a good review. I could go on. So I ask you: why should anyone believe another word the *Daily Mail* or *Mail on Sunday* say?

There are good reasons for taking what the *Mail* papers say with a pinch of salt, but the fact that they have made mistakes in the past is not a good enough reason to lose all trust in them altogether. Newspapers publish dozens of stories every day, all written by busy, fallible journalists. Mistakes will be made. That is a good reason for not simply assuming that everything you read in the papers is true, but it is insufficient reason for adopting a policy of global cynicism.

The *Mail*, however, is harsher on others than it is on itself. After the publication of the Phillips Report into the British government's handling of the mad cow disease crisis in 2000, it argued, in the editorial quoted above, that the mistakes Phillips highlighted made it difficult to trust the government or scientists ever again.

In fact, the Phillips Report mainly blamed bureaucratic delays and political handling for the failure to stop the spread of the disease, not scientists. The science behind the policy on BSE was inherently inconclusive, but it was up to politicians and civil servants to run risk assessments based on the evidence.

There seem to be, however, plenty of other examples of science either going wrong or leaving people confused: the disastrous side effects of drugs such as thalidomide, the conflicting reports about what it is healthy to eat, the use of DNA evidence to wrongly convict people of crimes they didn't commit, and technologies such as CFCs in fridges and lead in petrol which turned out to be destructive.

But although failing to learn from mistakes would be a scientific error, making them in the first place is not. Science proceeds by trial and error, and the evidence for any conclusion builds up slowly. One study can never, by itself, prove that wine is good for your heart, or that smoking kills you. Science reporting tends not to stress this. The media likes to present the latest study as though it were more certain than it is, and unfortunately, in order to seek publicity and funding, too many scientists now play the media's game. So when a finding turns out to be false, or in conflict with others, many members of the public think the science itself is confused.

Once the scientific community has settled on a broad consensus, more often than not it is right, and the benefits for the rest of us can be enormous. Sometimes drugs are not safe, but for everyone who has suffered because of unforeseen side effects, millions of people have been kept alive and healthy by medicines developed by men and women in white coats.

If trust means blind faith, then of course we should mistrust those who have shown themselves to be fallible, be they the media or the scientific community. But our scepticism needs to be proportionate. Too often people point to past failures as a reason for virtually discounting anything science or the press says.

What then is the right level of scepticism? It depends very much on the circumstances. Without trust, society could never function. But give too much of it too easily and you're sure to be let down.

Descartes said that it was 'prudent never to trust completely those who have deceived us even once'.[133] Even if he is right, how much partial trust can we place in those who are not 100 per cent reliable? Should you ever trust your partner again if you discover a long-running affair? Are some experts, such as economists, less reliable than others, such as biologists? Isn't it reasonable to want to know how many people die under the knife of a surgeon before letting her loose on your body?

See also

91. That's not what I said

Excessive literalness

Ahmadinejad did not say he was going to wipe Israel off the map because no such idiom exists in Persian.

Juan Cole, professor of history at the University of Michigan[134]

In October 2005, the Iranian President Mahmoud Ahmadinejad delivered one of the most notorious speeches in recent Middle East history. At a conference in Tehran called 'The World without Zionism', he said, 'Israel must be wiped off the map.' The remark was taken as indicative of the dangerous belligerence of the Iranian government and its threat to regional stability.

But is that what Ahmadinejad really said? Some Persian specialists insisted that a more accurate translation would have been, 'This regime that is occupying Jerusalem must vanish from the page of time.' Furthermore, they said, the remark should have been seen as a prophecy, not a threat, since the remark was an allusion to a phrase used by Ayatollah Khomeini, which saw the eventual overthrow of the current Israeli regime as being as inevitable as the earlier overthrow in Iran of the Shah's rule. The 'wiped off the map' translation, it is said, was a false one, used to justify American hawks who want tough action against Iran.

If this is true, however, why is it that all official translations of Ahmadinejad's statement, including references to it on his own website, refer to wiping Israel away? The *New York Times* quoted two bilingual Iranians who maintained that "wipe off" or "wipe away" is more accurate than "vanish" because the Persian verb is active and transitive.'

Confused? You should be. This debate is a vivid illustration of how sound reasoning is not achieved merely by logical and linguistic pedantry. One of the great contributions of European philosophy over the last century or so is the insight that under-standing the truth requires an attention to the social situatedness of statements, and not just their literal meaning.

As an informed citizen, how do you understand what Ahmadinejad's speech really signified? A close attention to his pre-cise words might help, but accurate translations alone are not enough. The most salient facts about this speech are, I would sug-gest, the following. First, Ahmadinejad delivered it to a fiercely anti-Israeli audience, who were ready to receive any message which supported their opposition to the legitimacy of Israel. Second, Ahmadinejad invoked Khomeini, whose regime fre-quently called for the destruction of Israel. Third, the speech was given during a time when many in Washington were calling for action against Iraq, so many in America were ready to give Ahmadinejad's words as negative a spin as possible. Only the fourth fact concerns his exact words, and that is that, however you interpret them, they contained no direct threat of Iranian action against Israel but clearly gave support to Israel's enemies, many of whom do use violence and some of which are funded by Iran.

What these facts add up to is that Ahmadinejad's was far from an innocent remark about the inevitable fate of all governments, but that the strength of reaction to it cannot be explained by the nature of his words alone: many people were looking for evidence of his extreme views on Israel.

Ahmadinejad seemed all too happy to give these people what they were looking for, which is an interesting fact in itself. (I should add that Professor Cole was sucked into a public debate about his translation against his will, and nothing he has said suggests to me that he thinks getting the translation exactly right clears everything up.)

Ahmadinejad's speech caused a major international row. But in many smaller ways, people often resort to the 'I didn't say that' defence when what matters is not their precise words but the manner and context of their utterance. To give a crude example, if I say that Fred is a nice guy and you snort derisively, you haven't said anything at all, but it would be ridiculous if you claimed 'I never said Fred wasn't nice.' Communication is not just about explicit speech.

Words require more than literal understanding, but there is a danger of reading too much into what people say. Is someone really sexist if he [*sic*] uses only masculine pronouns when referring to people who could be male or female? When is a refusal to comment a sign of guilt rather than a legitimate desire to preserve privacy? Are the dangers of over-interpretation greater than those of taking what people say at face value?

See also

92. The impossible flying machine

No rational explanation so not true

If you study medicine and pharmacology, you know [homeopathy] can't work.

Edzard Ernst, professor of complementary medicine[135]

In 1895, the president of the Royal Society of England declared, 'Heavier than air flying machines are impossible.' Lord Kelvin was one of the greatest scientists of his, or any, age. He developed the measure of absolute temperature and was the brains behind the laying of the first transatlantic telegraph cable. Fearless pioneers, however, are nothing if not bold, and although he was right about a great deal, on occasion he was spectacularly wrong.

Kelvin's famous remark about flight is often used by those who wish to claim, optimistically, that nothing is impossible. But it should be evident that the fact that some things which were thought to be impossible have turned out not to be does not demonstrate that we can actually do anything.

A better lesson can be learned from Kelvin's mistake with the help of a little speculation as to why he reached his conclusion: he simply had no way of accounting for how a heavier than air flying machine could work. Unable to see how they could fly, he concluded that they could not. The fact that birds are heavier than air should have been a clue that this line of

reasoning was suspect, but things are often obvious only in retrospect.

If this is broadly the reason why Kelvin went wrong, it
should alert us to the fact that the lack of a credible explanation
for something is not in itself a good enough reason to insist that
it can't happen. Present science is always incomplete and if we
conceive of the impossible solely within the framework of cur-
rently understood science, we're bound to rule out some things
that turn out to be possible after all.

That's why I'm not impressed by the argument frequently
used against homeopathy, reiterated by Edzard Ernst, that it
cannot work. The reason given is that the active ingredients in
homeopathic medicines are so diluted that there is simply not
enough of them left to have any effect, good or bad. In many
treatments, there are no molecules of the original substance left
at all, and the resulting 'medicine' is chemically just water.

This probably does explain why homeopathy doesn't
work. And let me be clear here: there is no credible scientific
evidence that it does. However, the case for its inefficacy
should not start from an assumption about what is and what is
not possible. Rather, homeopathy must be judged on its performance. The case against it should rest on its lack of results.
Having established that it doesn't work, it is then perfectly reasonable to explain its failure in terms of dilutions. But an
explanation as to why it *doesn't* work is not the same as a prior
ruling that it *can't*.

This matters, because I think it is entirely possible that
we will come across some medical practices which studies
show do work even though we can't see why they do. What's
more, the people who offer these treatments may give explanations that fly in the face of science. But if they work, they

work, and the challenge would then be to find out how they do.

In the case of homeopathy, the argument is especially harmful because it unnecessarily detracts from what should settle the issue. When people say it can't work, homeopaths blather on about 'the memory of water' and have been known to invoke quantum theory as some kind of potential explanation for this. This makes it all sound rather hi-tech and cutting edge, an attractive alternative to the staid conservatism of conventional medicine. But this is all beside the point: endless double-blind trials show it is useless, so the theoretical debates about the mechanism by which it works are moot.

This does not mean that our scientific understanding of what is impossible has no role at all to play in our assessment of evidence, however. Extraordinary claims require extraordinary evidence. If something goes against everything we know about science, a heightened degree of suspicion is entirely justified. The challenge is to have a mind that is not so closed that it becomes incapable of changing, and not so open that it ends up being filled with every crazy idea going. Pulling off that particular balancing act is not easy.

There should be a name for things that we have no reason to think would work, but do. I propose 'deodata' (*sing.* deodatum) named after Eumir Deodato for his jazz-funk rendition of Strauss's *Also Sprach Zarathustra*. It's easy enough compiling a frivolous list of deodata, but could there be more serious ones too? Placebos are one obvious contender. Conventional medicine accepts the placebo effect, but no one really knows how it works. Might other medical interventions be deodata too? Are there any apparently wacky, alternative or new-age practices that work, contrary to reason?

See also

93. Be thankful for bad employers

'It's better than nothing'

Although conditions in many of the [sweat]shops are admittedly wretched, people chose to work in the shops of their own free will, experts point out, because a lousy job is better than none at all.

National Center for Policy Analysis[136]

Sweatshops can make us feel very uncomfortable about the clothes we wear. We know that conditions in these factories, usually located in the developing world, are awful. We know that their workers often have few if any rights, receive measly pay and work in hazardous environments. If we think about it too much, we may even wonder if we are like modern-day slave-owners, enjoying the fruits of the labour of those who toil under conditions we would never accept for ourselves.

It can be very seductive, therefore, when someone comes up with an argument that tells us we shouldn't feel bad after all. Even better if that argument says some true things.

This argument comes courtesy of the National Center for Policy Analysis (NCPA), whose goal is 'to develop and promote private alternatives to government regulation and control, solving problems by relying on the strength of the competitive, entrepreneurial private sector'. Those not drawn towards neo-liberal free-market orthodoxy may feel suspicious of what such a body has to say, but the NCPA's argument needs to be judged on its merit, not its provenance.

Set aside for one moment the argument that the workers in these sweatshops chose to work there freely (which I discussed in §64). Focus instead on the main point, which is that 'a lousy job is better than none at all'. If we don't buy goods which come from sweatshops, it is claimed that the workers we are concerned about will be worse off.

The argument has a good pedigree. Much cited is Lucy Martinez-Mont's *Wall Street Journal* article 'Sweatshops Are Better than No Shops'[137] in which she wrote, 'Banning imports of child-made goods would eliminate jobs, hike labour costs, drive plants from poor countries and increase debt. Rich countries would sabotage Third World countries and deny poor children any hope of a better future.'

What Martinez-Mont says is true. The question is, what follows from it? What clearly doesn't follow is that we can carry on buying child-produced goods with impunity, as many (but not all) proponents of the argument would have you believe.

The reason for this is that the choice is not between the *status quo* and banning such imports. This is something most 'fairtrade' campaigners know full well. For example, the Maquila Solidarity Network advised, 'Don't promote a blanket boycott of all goods produced by child labour,' precisely on the grounds that simply withdrawing custom and leaving nothing in its place is harmful to those they want to help. The Ethical Trade Initiative base code prohibits 'new recruitment of child labour' and insists that member 'companies shall develop or participate in and contribute to policies and programmes which provide for the transition of any child found to be performing child labour to enable her or him to attend and remain in quality education until no longer a child'.

The point is simple. Poor working conditions may be better than nothing, but that does not justify us supporting poor working conditions. The alternative should not be nothing, but making things better. Parents who feed their child junk food cannot say that they should not be criticized because junk food is better than no food, because there is the option of offering proper food. 'Better than nothing' is no defence if you can do better still.

What if there is a genuine, forced choice between something bad, and nothing, which is even worse? A classic example is launching a military attack with unavoidable civilian casualties because the enemy is using innocent people as human shields. But if the assault is called off, the enemy could continue to launch deadly attacks against even more civilians. Isn't this a genuine case where doing something terrible really is better than doing nothing at all?

See also

94. No business for cardinals

'It's not for you to say'

It's none of his business. If a Scottish woman wants to have an abortion, it is up to her and her doctor.

Tim Street, director of the Family Planning
Association Scotland[138]

Cardinal Keith O'Brien is not the kind of Catholic who likes to express his opposition to abortion tactfully. In a sermon on the Catholic Church's annual 'Day for Life' he said, 'Let us build up within our society a generation of medical professionals who are unwilling to co-operate in the slaughter.' O'Brien, the leader of the Catholic Church in Scotland, described as 'lies and misinformation masquerading as compassion and truth' assurances given when the Abortion Act was passed in 1967 that terminations would be allowed only in exceptional circumstances.

If you have helped provide, performed, or had an abortion, these are harsh words: you are essentially being called a party to murder. You can almost feel the anger of Tim Street, director of the Family Planning Association Scotland, when he replied to O'Brien saying, 'It's none of his business.' But he's wrong.

There is a long tradition among supporters of abortion of arguing along the lines of Street, who said, 'If a Scottish woman wants to have an abortion, it is up to her and her doctor.' The general principle behind this seems to be that important life decisions are solely the concern of people who make them, and those required to help implement them.

This is too sweeping for several reasons. First of all, in the abortion case, it merely begs the question, because anti-abortionists believe that the unborn child has interests which are not sufficiently taken into account. For them, the argument that an abortion is solely a matter for the pregnant woman and her doctor is as abhorrent as claiming that murder is solely the business of the assassin and the person taking out the contract.

Second, even if we do believe outsiders have no right to intervene, they do have a right to help shape public attitudes and laws. We do not in general follow a policy whereby the only people entitled to express views on subjects are those directly affected by them. Governments would be foolish to consult only with the unemployed when deciding what benefits they should be given, or with the military when making decisions about wars. Of course, we should listen carefully to the people most directly involved in any issue, but that does not mean we then leave all decisions to them.

Third, at the very least people are entitled to express their opinions on matters that don't directly concern them. No one thinks that only those who have been burgled are entitled to an opinion on burglary, or that people who don't fly should have no say in whether aviation should be included in carbon trading.

Yet in some circumstances, people do come close to saying that only those who have first-hand experience of a subject are entitled to express an opinion on it. 'Unless you've been through it yourself, you can't know what you're talking about,' they say. True, but only in the tautological sense that you can only know what something feels like if you have felt it. But I can know – in the non-experiential sense – what heroin does to you without taking it. Indeed, it is only because we can have such knowledge that we avoid most of life's potential horrors.

Fourth, it is simply bizarre to say that the leader of a church should not express opinions about moral issues. I don't agree with the Catholic Church's teaching on most things, but I can see that giving moral guidance – even if it is wrong – is one of its clerics' core tasks. It may be that in general people should be careful before commenting on moral dilemmas they do not themselves face, but religious leaders and ethicists surely should not.

If we are to salvage a constructive point from this confused rhetoric, it is that we need to give due weight to knowledge, expertise and experience. Whether we usually do that is doubtful.

Whose opinions should count most in public debates about ethics? Are religious leaders really society's moral experts? Are criminologists consulted enough when politicians make penal policy? Is business given too big a say in how business is regulated? Everyone can contribute to society's debates, but shouldn't we listen more closely to some voices than others?

See also

95. They kill civilians, don't they?

Fallacy of accident

These days, the Americans routinely fire missiles into Fallujah and other dense urban areas; they murder whole families. If the word terrorism has any modern application, it is this industrial state terrorism.

John Pilger, journalist[139]

Few countries polarize opinion more than the USA. To many, it seems like a great champion of liberty and democracy. But to others, it is a bullying, neo-colonial empire, and the greatest threat to peace in the world today. Supporters of this second view often try to shatter the illusion that the USA is a benign force by arguing that many of its actions are morally equivalent to those of the rogue states and terrorist groups it frequently denounces.

One of the most popular variants of this line of argument compares American military campaigns with terrorism. John Pilger, a fierce opponent of American foreign policy, does just this when he says that the way America conducts its wars makes it guilty of state terrorism. Pilger has several reasons for this, but one that just doesn't seem to hold is that American bombings are acts of terror because they kill civilians.

This argument rests on a simple mistake, the fallacy of accident. This is when a general rule is applied to a case which is actually an exception to it. For instance, I like cats. But were I to think that because Mr Bigglesworth is a cat, I will like him, I would be wrong, because it turns out that Bigglesworth is a nasty piece of work. Similarly, I should not conclude that because evil people cause others pain, then my dentist is an evil person.

It is certainly true that terrorists kill civilians. But to conclude that therefore America is a terrorist state, because it too does things it knows will result in civilian deaths, is to go too far. By the same logic, General Motors is a terrorist company, because it produces things (cars) which it knows will result in the deaths of numerous innocent civilians.

By general consent, terrorists do more than cause civilians to die: they actively pursue this as a strategic goal. If you want to pin the label of terrorist on the US government, you've got to argue that when it fired rockets into Fallujah, a massacre of the innocents was the intention. That's certainly not what the US military says. They argue that their intention was to rout insurgents. However, because these forces mingled with civilians, there was no way to do this without killing civilians too. Whatever you think of the decision to attack them anyway, that is clearly not the same thing as killing innocents as a strategic goal. But this is what Pilger suggests when he uses the verb 'murder' – meaning intentional killing – to describe the bombing of Fallujah's civilian population.

What makes the mixing up of military and terrorist activity so egregious is that the difference in motivations is no secret. Al Qaeda never pretended that 9/11 was an attempt to attack the military, who unfortunately were hiding among civilians. Of course the intention was solely to massacre civilians, whereas even if some specific US military units have targeted civilians, the fact that this is not government policy should be obvious.

Of course, there are other arguments against launching military attacks in areas where there are many civilians: what I am saying is not a defence of any specific military action. All I'm trying to explain is why conflating the occupation forces with terrorists is not justified simply by the fact that both kill civilians.

To avoid the fallacy, one has to be careful to qualify the general statement which leads one to it. In this case, it is that terrorism involves not just the killing of civilians, but the targeting of them as a strategic goal. Such qualifications come more naturally if we get into the habit of remembering that few rules are without exception. If you always prefer fresh food to frozen, never trust a politician, maintain that power corrupts, think alternative medicine is bunkum, or believe good reasoning always trumps gut instinct – be careful: you may usually be right, but you wouldn't want to miss exceptions.

'Never say never' is a maxim which, if true, you should never say. But allowing for a little hyperbole, it's good advice, along with the less catchy 'Always avoid saying always.' Think about the all-encompassing beliefs you hold, those that include words like 'all', 'none' and 'every'. Do they not admit of exceptions? If so, what are they?

See also

96. What difference does it make?

Playing with game theory

> People who abstain in elections are making a rational decision. They are calculating that the benefit the result will bring them, multiplied by the probability that their vote will change the result, is smaller than the cost involved in making the effort to go to the polling station.
>
> Daniel Finkelstein, *The Times*[140]

In a world where our own actions are lost among those of billions of others, it is easy to think that little of what we do is worth the effort. You could cut your carbon emissions by turning your DVD player off standby, but since there will be 1,000 more cars on the streets of Beijing alone tomorrow, why bother?

Such pessimism is sometimes encouraged by game theory, and in particular its application by economists. Time and time again academics in this field show that, from a rational point of view, the benefits of many actions are so negligible that it is just not rational to perform them. Daniel Finkelstein offered a typically pithy example of this way of thinking in *The Times*, when he argued that voting is usually a waste of time.

Game theorists are hard, rational sorts and only a fool would dismiss their core empirical and statistical claims lightly. The problems come when people extrapolate from these claims to what we should do in real life.

Most problematically, game theory employs a notion of rationality which is extremely narrow and goal-orientated. In the theorists' universe, what is rational is what will actually enable you to achieve certain well-defined, specific goals. However, these goals do not necessarily match those of real people.

Take the election example. It might seem fair enough to say that the goal of voting is to affect the outcome, and if that is indeed the case, it can be shown that in anything but the most marginal of polls, you can't do that by voting, so it is irrational to do so. However, you may have very different goals, such as participating in a process which you think is the best system we have to produce accountable government. You can do this without suffering from any delusion that the result depends on you. Indeed, surely the whole point of a democracy is that no result depends on one person alone.

Even if you do want to vote to *affect* the outcome, this is not the same as believing that your vote must *critically determine* it. There is a subtle but important difference here: to believe, rationally, that your vote counts need not entail the belief that the result would be otherwise if you didn't cast it.

Nor is it the case that rational action should necessarily be defined in terms of immediate outcomes at all. Take the example of recycling. I may believe that it is important that we recycle much more than we do. At the same time, I may be aware that it makes no meaningful difference to the planet whether I do so or not. Nevertheless, it is rational to choose to behave in accordance with the values I proclaim: I want as many people as possible to recycle because together we make a difference, and so it is rational for me to follow my own maxim. Recycling is irrational only if one defines rationality so narrowly that it applies only to actions whose actual consequences matter.

In short, there are more reasons in heaven and earth than are dreamt of in some game theorists' philosophies.

Game theory can challenges comfortable assumptions about why we do what we do. Many people do like to think that the main reason they save carbon, recycle or vote is that, by doing so, they 'make a difference'. Although there may be other reasons for carrying on, isn't it the case that it is harder to be motivated by more indirect rationales than directly affecting outcomes? Once you accept that it doesn't make a difference whether your bottle goes in the bin or the recycler, aren't your reasons for doing your bit psychologically less compelling, even if they are justified? And since we are more motivated by psychology than logic, does that perhaps mean we should spread the noble lie that every little bit really does help?

See also

97. Attack of the killer shrubs

Ridicule and the ridiculous

> The war on drugs was weird enough because it was a war
> on plants, which I found quite odd. But the whole concept
> of a war on terror is absurd. How can you declare war on
> an abstract, on a notion?
>
> Mark Thomas, comedian[141]

Comedy has always been one of the most potent modes of political and social commentary and polemic. In Britain, for example, comedians such as Ben Elton in the eighties and Rory Bremner and Mark Steel in the present day have been praised as some of the most effective critics of the politicians of their time. Michael Moore in the US and Mark Thomas in the UK have recently pioneered a popular new hybrid of investigative journalism and comedy.

The comedian's skills, however, do not always lend themselves to the kind of subtle analysis required by good political commentary. The political comedian is the master of ridicule, but it is easy to forget that what has been made to *look* ridiculous may not in fact *be* ridiculous.

Take Mark Thomas's swipes at the war on drugs and the war on terror. Not bad gags, I would say. But do they add up to serious criticisms of either? Hardly. Consider the war on drugs first. The joke works because it makes us imagine an absurd armed struggle in which the enemy is a plant. But, of course, no one involved in the war on drugs thinks they are actually going into battle with plants. In fact, they probably don't even think that they're engaged in a war in the conventional sense at all. The 'war on drugs' is merely a kind of metaphor or shorthand for a policy of working to eliminate the supply and use of drugs.

What the joke does is take the phrase 'war on drugs', interpret it in a deliberately over-literal way, and then show how, on that interpretation, such a war is ridiculous. But this is a far cry from having shown that the 'war' itself is ridiculous. In fact, the joke cannot do this because it doesn't even begin to address what the war on drugs is really about. However, comedy is in the timing, and gags, unlike careful arguments, follow each other quickly. It is easy in our laughter to think that we are finding drugs policy ridiculous, rather than finding a clever joke funny.

Moore's ridicule is also often far from incisive. In *Fahrenheit 9/11* he mocked George Bush for taking a long time to think about what to say when he was informed about the attack on the Twin Towers. But if you stop sniggering and think about it, why was it bad to hold back? Wouldn't it have been worse if Bush had just stood up and said the first thing that came into his head?

If all this sounds like taking comedy too seriously then it should be remembered that many comedians are very earnest about their political objectives. They are very articulate and persuasive spokespeople for their causes, whose fans often seem to think that they have spoken truth to power. Their work can be excellent, and the jokes hit upon uncomfortable truths. Both Michael Moore and Mark Thomas in particular have produced some searching and disturbing work. But both ridicule some things that aren't actually ridiculous and make us see problems in the wrong places. Comedy can reveal the truth, but it can also make us miss it.

How many classic satires actually hit their targets? Set aside their artistic and comic merits for a moment and ask yourself, did *Dr Strangelove* really tell us anything profound about the Cold War? Did *The Life of Brian* reveal the absurdity of organized religion? Did Robert Altman's *The Player* or *Prêt a Porter* really capture the follies of Hollywood and fashion? Sometimes the answer is a resounding yes, but very often the old adage that something is funny because it is true is neither true nor funny.

See also

98. Too much of nothing is not enough

Quantity over quality

There've been too many reports of spectres and ghostly phenomena to be ignored: Something must be out there!

Tom Ogden, *The Complete Idiot's Guide to Ghosts and Hauntings*[142]

The 9/11 conspiracy theory detailed in the documentary *Loose Change* is powerful stuff.[143] For ninety minutes you are bombarded with evidence which, it is claimed, all points to the attacks on the Twin Towers being an inside job, designed to create a 'new Pearl Harbor', thus legitimizing the neo-conservative agenda.

Like most people, if I am presented with a huge quantity of evidence such as this, my judgement is at least temporarily swayed. It shouldn't be, since quantity is not the same as quality. No amount of bad evidence can ever build up to a good overall case: it is overwhelming only in the wrong sense.

Loose Change is an excellent example of the power of quantity over quality of evidence. We are told that in 1962, the Joint Chiefs of Staff presented a report to Secretary of Defense Robert McNamara suggesting terrorist attacks were staged in Guantanamo Bay to provide a pretext for attacking Cuba. Sound familiar? But that proves nothing except that faking terrorist attacks had been considered at some time in the past. So what? It has nothing to do with events forty years later.

Next, in 1984 a remote controlled Boeing 720 was flown for sixteen hours and then crash landed by Nasa. Again, so what? We all know that planes can be flown by remote control. Then, in 1997 the cover of FEMA's Emergency Response to Terrorism Self-Study depicted the World Trade Center in crosshairs (a type of weapons sight). Again, so what? If America was to be attacked by terrorists, the World Trade Center was an obvious target. Do the film-makers think that FEMA's graphic designer was in on the plot?

All this is just in the first few minutes. And so it goes on, for nearly ninety more. Nothing plus nothing equals nothing, but for some reason, when bad evidence mounts up, we seem to think that makes it better. Could it really be a coincidence that the US had considered faking a terrorist attack, had experimented with drone aircraft, and had even believed the World Trade Center as a target? No, because it isn't a coincidence: these are all things you would have expected the US government to have thought about at some point in the past.

Evidence for ghosts and other supernatural events accumulates in the same way. *The Complete Idiot's Guide to Ghosts and Hauntings* is well named, because it does not follow, as its author claims, that 'Something must be out there!' just because there have been 'too many reports of spectres and ghostly phenomena'. Quality, not quantity, counts. A handful – perhaps even one – properly verified encounter with a ghost would prove they exist. But no number of inconclusive anecdotes adds up to a case. Indeed, it could even work the other way around: the fact that thousands of alleged ghost sightings have been reported and investigated and yet none has been proven to be real suggests that ghosts simply don't exist.

It is not only the case that no amount of zeros adds up to a one, it is also true that probabilities do not accrue by addition. If you have ten pieces of evidence each pointing to the same outcome with 10 per cent probability, that does not mean that together they make the outcome 100 per cent probable. Rather it is the case that each piece of evidence independently reaches the same conclusion: that the event is unlikely. Intuitively, however, we tend to assume that dozens of pieces of evidence which suggest something might be true together suggest it probably is.

By extension, if we have ten ways of working out how probable it is that a train will crash, and every one comes up with an answer between 55 and 65 per cent, we have good reason for thinking the train will probably crash, but still with only around a 60 per cent probability.

I could say more, but since the point is that it's not the number of reasons that count, but how good they are, I think I'll stop now.

What other examples might there be of people being blinded by volume of evidence? Mohammed Al Fayed has gathered lots of evidence that Princess Diana was murdered. There is lots of evidence that smoking causes cancer. Homeopaths can point you to numerous studies which say their treatments work. Which of these cases contains quality as well as quantity of evidence?

See also

99. The real thing

The no-true-Scotsman move

We know that no real alcoholic ever recovers control.

The AA Big Book[144]

'Extremism is not the true voice of Islam,' Tony Blair said in a speech at the Foreign Policy Centre in March 2006. So what is that genuine voice? 'It is, as ever, to be found in the calm, but too often unheard beliefs of the many Muslims, millions of them the world over, including in Europe, who want what we all want: to be ourselves free and for others to be free also; who regard tolerance as a virtue and respect for the faith of others as part of our own faith.'

It would be nice if this were true, especially for those calm Muslims Blair talked about, fed up with being tarred with the same brush as suicide bombers. However, not everyone agrees. Mufti Zubair Dudha taught children and young people at his Islamic Tarbiyah Academy in Dewsbury, and in a foreword to a translated pamphlet in 1996 he wrote, 'No learned person and no true Muslim can deny the benefits, fruits and blessings of physical jihad for the course of Allah.'

According to Blair, a Roman Catholic, the Muslim Dudha can't be a true Muslim. According to Dudha, it's Blair who's talking nonsense. Who are we to believe?

The answer is neither. When phrases like 'true Muslim' are

used in this way they are practically meaningless. There are some senses in which one can talk about true and false Muslims. Someone merely pretending to follow Islam would not be a true believer, for example. There might also be some fringe cults so far removed from the rest of Islam that they could legitimately be disowned by other Muslims. But Muslims come in many shapes and forms, from suicide bombers to secular Muslims whom most of their coreligionists would regard as apostates. When someone tries to say what true Muslims are like, all they are really doing is telling you what version of Islam they approve of.

It's the same for other religions. Some will say that no true Christian would condone homosexuality, perhaps quoting St Paul: 'Men committed indecent acts with other men, and received in themselves the due penalty for their perversion' (Romans 1:27). Others would say no true Christian would condemn anyone on the basis of their God-given sexuality, questioning the interpretation of the very few New Testament passages that touch on homosexuality. But again, Christians just disagree and saying what 'true' ones should think is simply to claim a bogus authority for the view you take.

Alcoholics Anonymous is notorious for its claims about what makes a 'true alcoholic'. AA says that no alcoholic can ever become a controlled drinker and total abstinence is the only cure. The problem is that there seem to be many counter examples: problem drinkers who learned to moderate their intake. But to AA, this can't count as counter evidence, since these people are either not true alcoholics by definition or their relapse just hasn't happened yet.

This way of arguing was called the 'No-true-Scotsman move' by the philosopher Antony Flew, who used his own fictitious example of a Scotsman who read about the antics of a sex maniac and said, 'No Scot would do such a thing!' When, the following week, he read a story which seemed to contradict him, he stood his ground, saying 'No *true Scotsman* would do such a thing!'[145] Flew thought this a bad argumentative move, and would any true rationalist disagree?

One reason why the no-true-Scotsman move is so tempting is because none of us likes to think that we keep company with people we find abhorrent. There are all sorts of things I would like to think no true philosopher would do, but many have evidently done them. I suspect it may also be the case that some true animal lovers do, through ignorance, treat their pets badly; that some true film lovers actually liked Julie Delpy's execrable directorial debut, *2 Days in Paris*; and that true love doesn't always last. Are there any things that true members of your tribe might do, loath though you would be to admit it?

See also

100. The last word

Complacent superiority

Who do we think we are, we guardians of good sense and rationality? In this book, I have tried to detail various ways in which arguments or points are made badly but often persuasively. Does that mean I think my own arguments are made well? If so, is that justified confidence or terrible arrogance?

Actually, I don't think I am immune to the mistakes I have catalogued here. I may even have made a few of them (or others) in these very pages. That is not a fatalistic admission that none of us can ever be more rational or consistent than any other. It is rather a reminder that the pursuit of noble ends, such as truth or goodness, is difficult and bound to be accompanied by error. However, when one puts oneself on the side of the angels it is all too easy to start believing that one has sprouted wings. The result can then be complacent superiority: the belief that one is 'good' or 'rational' and therefore immunized against wickedness or poor reasoning. If one starts to believe that, or adopt it as an unconscious assumption, then one is in danger of falling into just the kind of badness or ignorance one is supposed to be against.

I have, unfortunately, seen it happen with trained philosophers, who grow to assume that they have critical thinking skills denied to the rest of the world, but then fail to use them correctly. They sometimes commit what I'd call the 'fallacy fallacy': believing that because they can identify the form of a logical mistake in an argument, they can therefore dismiss it out of hand.

One good example was a philosopher who ridiculed the way in which the editor of the *Lancet*, Dr Richard Horton, backtracked on his decision to publish a controversial article by Andrew Wakefield which suggested a link between the MMR vaccine and autism. The reason Horton gave was that the funding for the study used for the article was not disclosed and its source created a conflict of interests for Wakefield.

The philosopher thought Horton had committed a version of the genetic fallacy: a belief has to be assessed on its own merits, not on those of its origins (see §28). But in this case it was wrong simply to lift this principle out of the critical thinking textbooks and apply it blindly. Experimenter bias is a very important factor in science research and that's why it really does matter that there is full disclosure about who has funded and set up a study. It should not have been a hard point to spot, but the philosopher's over-confidence in his ability to identify bad reasoning led him to succumb to it himself.

There are two important things to remember if we are to avoid falling into the trap of over-confidence. The first is simple vigilance. Never assume your arguments are rational; always scrutinize your own reasoning for signs of sloppiness. The second is recognizing that the lines which divide the clever and the stupid, the good and the poor argument, are rarely sharp.

It also has to be admitted that even the most rational of arguments are not free from rhetorical flourish. There is nothing wrong with this. Apart from anything else, our texts would be very dry if they always aspired to be as neutral and humourless as is possible. Hardly anything we read or write is entirely free of all rhetorical content. Rhetoric can make good arguments more persuasive and following them more enjoyable. It is only when rhetoric is in the service of poor reasoning that it becomes a problem.

Nonetheless, rhetoric is not the same as rational argumentation, so those who aspire to be on the side of reason need to remember not only that they are fallible but that they too use some of the tricks of persuasion they are only too keen to criticize in their adversaries.

My hope is that this book will help you to be more sensitive to the myriad ways in which bad arguments are made persuasively. To apply it to the real world, however, requires not so much memorizing a catalogue of fallacies but adopting a habit of constructive, thoughtful scepticism in our reading and listening. If we do this, the bad arguments will identify themselves, and we will become better, if still imperfect, thinkers.

See also

Everything

Answer to question on page 49
(16: The gambler's fallacy)

Neither is more likely to win. Because each toss of the coin is a 50/50 bet, Jim's random choice of head or tails is no more or less likely to be right than Jack's choice, based on a mistaken idea of probability. Neither thinking that there is a pattern, nor knowing that there isn't, can change the odds.

Answer to question on page 65
(no: The gambler's fallacy)

Notes

1 'This much I know', *Observer Magazine*, 16 June 2002
2 'Woolly writing creates new poetry', BBC News Online, 4 December 2002, http://news.bbc.co.uk/1/hi/england/2541761.stm
3 *The Quantum Self: Human Nature and Consciousness Defined by the New Physics*, Danah Zohar (Bloomsbury, 1990)
4 'Physics on the brain', Susan Blackmore, *New Scientist*, 5 January 1991
5 Interview given to TF1 and France 2, 1 March 2003. Transcript by French Embassy in UK, www.ambafrance-uk.org/Iraq-Interview-given-by-M-Jacques.html
6 'British Prime Minister Defends Arms To Israel', Neil Roberts, *Daily Mirror*, 25 July 2002
7 'Life is for living', David Cohen, *Candis*, November 2006
8 'Clinic assists doctor's suicide', BBC News Online, 24 January 2006, http://news.bbc.co.uk/1/hi/health/4625538.stm
9 *Existentialism and Humanism*, Jean-Paul Sartre, trans. Philip Mairet (Methuen, 1973)
10 'Sign writer', David Smith, the *Observer*, 20 June 2004
11 'The Comprehensive Spending Reviews, First Report of Session 2007–08', House of Commons Treasury Select Committee
12 Joseph Rowntree Foundation child poverty update, www.jrf.org.uk/child-poverty
13 'A league table of child poverty in rich nations', Innocenti Report Card No.1, June 2000, UNICEF Innocenti Research Centre
14 Donald Rumsfeld, Defense Department briefing, 12 February 2002
15 'Ask Emma', Emma Mitchell, *Guardian*, 7 September 2002
16 *Wild: An Elemental Journey*, Jay Griffiths (Hamish Hamilton, 2007) pp. 47–8; Shape-shifting references, p. 82
17 Leader column, *Economist*, 26 July 2003
18 'Report: Islamophobia makes British Muslims feel increasingly "isolated" in their own country', Maxine Frith, *Independent*, 22 November 2004
19 'After Debate, Clinton Keeps Chipping Away at Obama', Jason Horowitz, *New York Observer*, 19 November 2007
20 *Spirit and Destiny* magazine, February 2003
21 'Britons unconvinced on evolution', 26 January 2006, http://news.bbc.co.uk/1/hi/sci/tech/4648598.stm

Notes

22 'Open predictions', BBC Sport Online, 16 July 2006, http://news.bbc.co.uk/sport1/hi/golf/5196078.stm

23 'You voted for this ridiculous war, Reid. So go fight it', Martin Samuel, *The Times*, 21 August 2007

24 Kim Catcheside, *BBC 1 O'Clock News*, 15 September 1998

25 'I know where I stood on abortion. But I had to rethink', Miranda Sawyer, *Observer*, 8 April 2007

26 'The importance of being earnest', Craig McLean, *Guardian Weekend*, 28 May 2005

27 *Life of Samuel Johnson*, James Boswell (1791)

28 *Daily Life in Johnson's London*, Richard B. Schwartz (University of Wisconsin Press, 1984)

29 'Now the Pentagon tells Bush: climate change will destroy us', *Observer*, 22 February 2004

30 'Fast forward into trouble', Cathy Scott-Clark and Adrian Levy, *Guardian*, 14 June 2003

31 'A world like any other', Richard Eyre, *Guardian Review,* 21 August 2004

32 'This ban will not stop us', Brian Eno, *Guardian*, 6 October 2007

33 'Stars join antiwar protest', Mark Davies, BBC News Online, 21 January 2003, http://news.bbc.co.uk/1/hi/uk_politics/2681243.stm

34 'Oooh duckie we got lucky', Andy Russell, *Sun*, 12 November 2005

35 *Manchester Metro*, 13 September 2002

36 'If God died for all of us, it is not ours to decide who is fit to live', Cardinal Cormac Murphy-O'Connor, *Sunday Telegraph*, 27 March 2005

37 'What's in your basket?', *Observer Food Monthly,* August 2004

38 'TV chef Floyd was three times over drink-drive limit', Richard Savill, *Daily Telegraph*, 24 November 2004

39 President's remarks to the Coalition for Medicare Choices, 17 May 2002, www.whitehouse.gov/news/releases/2002/05/20020517-8.html

40 William Hague, Conservative Party 2001 General Election manifesto

41 'Theistic critiques of Atheism', William Lane Craig, in *The Cambridge Companion to Atheism*, ed. Michael Martin (Cambridge University Press, 2007) p. 73

42 'Pill row takes new turn', BBC News Online, 11 December 2000, http://news.bbc.co.uk/1/hi/health/1065971.stm

43 'No-sex programmes "not working"', BBC News Online, 2 August 2007, http://news.bbc.co.uk/1/hi/health/6927733.stm

44 'After the Promise: The STD Consequences of Adolescent Virginity Pledges', Bruckner, Hannah and Peter Bearman, *Journal of Adolescent Health*, 36 (2005), 271–8

45 *Today*, BBC Radio Four, 28 November 2006

Notes

46 *Today*, BBC Radio Four, 20 December 2004

47 'I would not have voted for Iraq war, says Howard', David Cracknell and David Leppard, *Sunday Times*, 18 July 2004

48 'The Right Way in Iraq', John Edwards, *Washington Post*, 13 November 2005

49 *Today*, BBC Radio Four, 25 June 2007

50 'Now Charles backs coffee cure for cancer', Jo Revill, *Observer*, 27 June 2004

51 'Initial Severity and Antidepressant Benefits: A Meta-Analysis of Data Submitted to the Food and Drug Administration', Kirsch I., Deacon B. J., Huedo-Medina T. B., et al., *PLoS Med*, 2008; 5(2)

52 'Why men rape', Randy Thornhill and Craig Palmer, *The Sciences* (The New York Academy Of Sciences, January/February 2000)

53 Ronald Reagan, 1987 State of the Union Address

54 'Firearms: A civil liberties issue?' BBC News Online, 6 March 2001, http://news.bbc.co.uk/1/hi/world/americas/326106.stm

55 *Infinitely Demanding*, Simon Critchley (Verso, 1997), though the phrase 'ought implies cannot' was said in an interview with *The Philosophers' Magazine*, issue 40, 1st quarter 2008

56 *Therapy Culture*, Frank Furedi (Routledge, 2004), p. 204

57 Address to a Joint Session of Congress and the American People, 20 September 2001, www.whitehouse.gov/news/releases/2001/09/20010920-8.html

58 'Diana "foresaw death crash"', *Evening Standard* front-page headline, 20 October 2003

59 'Intelligent Design in Biology', Phillip E. Johnson, *Think*, Issue 11, autumn 2005

60 *Big Issue in the North*, 1996

61 David Hume, *An Enquiry concerning Human Understanding* [1748]

62 'Primal life force under the ice', David G. Anderson, *Times Higher Education Supplement*, 8 August 2003

63 'Kennedy criticises terror tactics', BBC News Online, 23 November 2004, http://news.bbc.co.uk/1/hi/uk_politics/4035659.stm

64 Erich von Däniken official website, http://www.daniken.com/e/

65 *Today*, BBC Radio Four, 15 December 2003

66 'Compatible compatriots', interview by Kristine McKenna, *Los Angeles Times*, 22 December 1997

67 Professor Robert Hazell, *Public Servant*, December 2007

68 Frédéric Beigbeder, *£9.99* (Picador, 2002)

69 Fox News, 3 October 2005, www.foxnews.com/story/0,2933,171007,00.html

70 'Call him Mr Loophole', Steve Boggan, *Guardian*, 27 January 2006

Notes

71 'The Real Root Causes of Violent Crime: The Breakdown of Marriage, Family, and Community', Patrick F. Fagan, The Heritage Foundation (www.heritage.org), Backgrounder #1026, 17 March, 1995

72 'Call for Ireland to be GM free', Press Association, 9 June 2003

73 *Rocky Mountain News*, CO, 21 May 2003

74 *Toronto Star*, Canada, 19 May 2003

75 CNN, 12 October 2006

76 'The Boss, Tower of faith and loyalty', Archie Dunham, written with David Leonhardt, *New York Times*, 23 February 2000

77 'House Drops Genocide Measure', CBS News, 20 October 2000, www.cbsnews.com/stories/2000/10/11/world/main240298.shtml

78 'Writer repeats Turk deaths claim', BBC News Online, 23 October 2005, http://news.bbc.co.uk/1/hi/world/europe/4369562.stm

79 'EU threatens to ban vitamin supplements', Geoffrey Lean, *Independent,* 10 March 2002

80 2003 campaign (Source: *Economist*, 29 March 2003)

81 Reported comment to friend, Sky News, 22 March 2007

82 'Kiddies' cornucopia is not all it seems', Neil Collins, *Daily Telegraph*, 21 April 2003

83 Mark Easton, BBC home affairs correspondent, *10 O'Clock News*, 1 June 2007

84 'The bookseller', Nicholas Clee, *Guardian*, 13 March 2004

85 'Mothers are "happier" having a job', BBC News Online, 12 December 2007, http://news.bbc.co.uk/1/hi/business/7140093.stm

86 'Prejudice put down to "ignorance"', John Knox, BBC News Online, 11 December 2007, http://news.bbc.co.uk/1/hi/scotland/7138538.stm

87 'Broadband customers put on hold', BBC News Online, 6 December 2007, http://news.bbc.co.uk/1/hi/technology/7129012.stm

88 'England's pupils feel less safe', BBC News Online, 30 November 2007, http://news.bbc.co.uk/1/hi/education/7121824.stm

89 'Cigarette giant to dent cancer links', Jamie Doward, *Observer*, 5 October 2003

90 *Hen's Teeth and Horse's Toes*, Stephen Jay Gould (WW Norton, 1994)

91 *Inventing Temperature: Measurement and Scientific Progress*, Hasok Chang (Oxford University Press, 2004)

92 'Who stole all your friends?', Carol Sarler, *The Times*, 26 June 2006

93 'A friendlier brand of reality show', AA Gill, *Sunday Times*, 1 April 2007

94 'Poor man's hero', Nick Gillespie, *Reason* magazine, December 2003

95 'Berg's murder is not fault of U.S.', A. J. Magnuson, *The Stanford Daily*, 14 May 2004

96 'Slain man thought he could "help"', CBS News Online, 11 May 2004

Notes

97   Book endorsement on paperback cover of George Monbiot's *Captive State* (Pan Books, 2001)

98   Boris Johnson, 23 February 2006, www.boris-johnson.com/archives/2006/02/post_1.php

99   Leader, *Economist*, 29 November 2007

100 'Do stop behaving as if you are God, Professor Dawkins', Alister McGrath, *Daily Mail*, 9 February 2007

101 Naomi Klein, FAQ at nologo.org website, since removed

102 'Gene-juggling', Mary Midgley, *Philosophy*, 54 (October 1979)

103 Bill Clinton, televised White House press conference, 26 January 2003

104 'My answer', Billy Graham, syndicated column, www.billygraham.org/MyAnswer_Article.asp?ArticleID=1864

105 Peter Hitchens column, *Mail on Sunday*, 10 July 2005

106 *Lectures and Conversations on Aesthetics, Psychology and Religious Belief*, Ludwig Wittgenstein (ed. C. Barrett), (Blackwell, 1966)

107 *Stupid White Men ... and Other Sorry Excuses for the State of the Nation!*, Michael Moore (Penguin Books, 2004), p. 132

108 'Why peace is a conjuror's trick', Tom Palaima, *Times Higher Education Supplement*, 12 December 2003

109 'Obama again stirs up rivals with statement on use of nukes', Anne E. Kornblut, *Washington Post* election blog, 2 August 2007, http://blog.washingtonpost.com/the-trail/2007/08/02/obama_rules_out_nuclear_weapon.html

110 *Enough Rope*, ABC TV Australia, 4 October 2004

111 'Birth – the ultimate miracle', *Guardian*, 20 December 2003

112 *The Book of Luck – Brilliant Ideas for Creating Your Own Success and Making Life Go Your Way*, Heather Summers and Anne Watson (Capstone, 2004), p. 18

113 'No such thing as luck', Julia Stewart, *Independent*, 23 November 2004

114 Cited by Masters of Foxhounds Association, www.mfha.org.uk/index.php?option=com_content&task=blogcategory&id=26&Itemid=48

115 'The Absurdity of Life Without God', Chapter 2 of *Reasonable Faith*, www.bethinking.org/resource.php?ID=129

116 'I refuse to believe the McCanns are guilty', Allison Pearson, *Daily Mail*, 12 September 2007

117 Alistair Darling, interviewed by Andrew Marr, *Sunday AM*, BBC One, 2 April 2006

118 Lord Davies of Oldham, Hansard, 30 January 2007

119 Opening speech at 10th meeting of SEECP, José Manuel Barroso, 11 May 2007, http://europa.eu/rapid/searchAction.do

120 'Students need to know what sort of dangerous people are out there', *Guardian*, 26 November 2007

Notes

121 'Ian Paisley – what a laugh', Deborah Ross, *Independent*, 22 May 1998

122 'Obama: My wife sees need for rural gun ownership', John McCormick, *Baltimore Sun* blog (http://weblogs.baltimoresun.com), 25 November 2007

123 *The Unnatural Nature of Science*, Lewis Wolpert (Faber, 1992)

124 'Big-tobacco foe: fast food nearly as addictive as drugs; lawyer serves notice he'll sue to force dietary warnings – NRN National Report – John Banzhaf', Milford Prewitt, *Nation's Restaurant News*, 26 May 2003

125 'More than 50 dangerous pesticides found in British food', Geoffrey Lean, *Independent on Sunday*, 27 February 2005

126 'What's eating Jack?', *Observer Music Monthly*, November 2004

127 Research commissioned for *Flat Earth News*, Nick Davies (Chatto and Windus, 2008)

128 'Without prejudice', Nick Cohen, *Observer*, 5 December 2004

129 *We Become Silent – The Last Days Of Health Freedom,* dir. Kevin P. Miller (2006)

130 'US to rate its allies on their treatment of Jews', David Rennie, *Daily Telegraph*, 13 October 2004

131 Editorial, *Daily Mail*, 27 October 2000

132 A catalogue of such stories can be found at www.mediauk.com/newspapers/news/13700/daily-mail

133 First meditation of *Meditations on First Philosophy*, René Descartes [1641]

134 'Just how far did they go, those words against Israel?' Ethan Bronner, *New York Times*, 11 June 2006

135 'The alternative professor', Sarah Boseley, *Guardian*, 25 September 2003

136 National Center for Policy Analysis, Month In Review: Trade, June 1996, www.ncpa.org/pd/monthly/pd696r.html

137 'Sweatshops are better than no shops', Lucy Martinez-Mont, *Wall Street Journal*, 25 June 1996

138 '"Lies masquerading as truth" – Cardinal on abortion laws', *The Scotsman*, 30 May 2007

139 'Time to recognise state terrorism', John Pilger, antiwar.com, 17 September 2004, www.antiwar.com/orig/pilger.php?articleid=3592

140 'I don't care if you don't vote', Daniel Finkelstein, *The Times*, 12 December 2007

141 Mark Thomas, *The Big Issue*, 2–8 December 2002

142 *The Complete Idiot's Guide to Ghosts and Hauntings*, Tom Ogden (Alpha Books, 1999), p. 3

143 *Loose Change* documentary, www.loosechange911.com

144 *The AA Big Book* (4th edn online), p. 30, www.alcoholics-anonymous.org.uk/BigBook/

145 *Thinking about Thinking*, Antony Flew (Fontana, 1975), p. 47

Index

Index

Index

Index

Index

food (continued)
  fast, 56, 260–2
  fresh, 21, 240, 298
  GM, 31–3, 279
  junk, 292
  labelling, 123
  and pesticides, 264–5
  supplements, 179–80, 273–4
football, 80, 88, 107–8, 129, 185
Foreign Policy Centre, 309
foresight, 128–30
Fox, Dr Liam, 98–9
fox-hunting, 76, 241
France, 7–8, 176
Fraser, Rev. Giles, 236
fraud, 135–6
free markets, 87, 214, 290
free speech, 139–40
free will, 246
freedom fighters, 59
Freeman, Nick, 160
French Resistance, 223
Freud, Sigmund, 131
friends, 196
Frith, Maxine, 34
Frost, Martyn, 79
fruit juices, 110
Furedi, Frank, 122–3

gambler's fallacy, 47–9
game theory, 299–301
gay rights, 100
gender, 30, 209
  inequality, 275
General Motors, 197
generosity, 185
genetic enhancement, 155
genetic fallacy, 85–7, 313
genocide, 175–6
geography, 83
Gerhardi, Gillian, 13–15

Gerson Therapy, 110–11
ghosts, 305–7
Gill, A. A., 197
global warming, 69, 97, 118, 197,
    226–8
  see also climate change
God, 6, 24, 35, 45, 96, 146, 158,
    171, 173, 244–5
  belief in, 211–12, 275
  and killing, 262
  separation from, 221
  son of, 126, 208
God Delusion, The (Dawkins), 211
gods, 28, 144
Goebbels, Joseph, 268
Goldacre, Ben, 206
Goldfrapp, 205
golf, 48–9
Google, 144–5, 267
Goosen, Retief, 48–9
Gore, Al, 167
Gould, Stephen Jay, 194
Graham, Rev. Billy, 220–1
gravity, 3
Greece, ancient, 150
Green Party, 208
Greenspan, Alan, 252
Greenstock, Sir Jeremy, 147–8
Griffin, Nick, 161, 209
Griffiths, Jay, 28–9
Guantanamo Bay, 305
guarana, 182
Guardian, 70, 192, 236, 270–1
guilt by association, 82–4
Gulf War veterans, 137
gun controls, 120, 140, 257
gypsies, 64

Hack, Damon, 47–8
Hague William, 91
haikus, 4

Index

Index

Index